Beyond

Finding Belonging and Leading with Purpose

by

Leela Bassi

Published by Mabel and Stanley
Publishing – July 2025

© All Rights Reserved

BEYOND THE ICE

Disclaimer

This book is intended to serve as a guide to leadership with integrity, and to promote principles of diversity and inclusion. It outlines 11 core principles designed to support personal and professional growth as a leader. Whilst these principles are based on widely recognised best practices, extensive author experience and thoughtful reflection, they are not intended to be definitive or universally applicable in every context.

The guidance provided herein does not guarantee specific results. Leadership development is a deeply personal journey influenced by a variety of factors, including but not limited to, individual effort, situational variables, and external circumstances. Success in applying these principles will depend on how they are interpreted and implemented by each reader.

The author and publisher make no representations or warranties with respect to the outcomes achieved through the use of the content in this book. Readers are encouraged to exercise critical thinking and adapt the material in a manner that aligns with their unique values, contexts, and objectives.

BEYOND THE ICE

Dedication

This book is dedicated to the ones who stayed. The ones who left. The ones who returned.

And to my family, who made the journey home possible.

Matteo, The love of my life. Thank you for being my calm in every storm. You are my rock, my fortress, and my steady strength. Thank you for believing in me even when I doubted myself; I am forever grateful.

To ***Elisa,*** your creativity is bold, vibrant, and limitless. Your joyful spirit, your energy, and your love for what you do remind me that passion has power. Whatever you dream, you can be; and your journey is just beginning. Never doubt that your spark can light up places no one else dares to go.

To ***Stefano,*** you've shown us what quiet strength looks like. Your courage, discipline, and willingness to grow inspire me deeply. You've turned challenges into stepping stones and that is true resilience. Keep going, keep rising, keep believing.

Together, you are my **why**, my **pride**, and my **greatest legacy**.

BEYOND THE ICE

BEYOND THE ICE

In *Beyond the Ice*, Leela takes you on a deeply personal and professional journey through some of life's most extreme conditions, from the frozen expanse of the Arctic to the deep ache of growing up feeling different. Part memoir, part leadership guide, this powerful book redefines what it means to lead with courage, connection, and clarity.

Drawing on stories from the boardroom, the mountains, and everything in between, Leela explores resilience, identity, belonging, and the unseen strength it takes to lead from within. You will enter workplaces where inclusion is more than policy, it is lived, challenged, and earned. And you will see how true leadership is built not in titles or applause, but in the steady, consistent ways we show up for ourselves and others.

This book is for anyone who has ever questioned their place, felt like an outsider, or longed to lead with more intention and heart. It's a call to stop performing, start listening, and lead in a way that reflects who you truly are.

Because the greatest journeys do not just take us across landscapes.

They bring us home to ourselves.

BEYOND THE ICE

Reviews for Beyond the Ice

"This read is a must for anyone who sees themselves as a leader. It reminded me that real leadership is not about titles or accolades, but about how we show up, how we act, and the impact we have on others."

Gina Atkinson – Military Veteran

"This book is so much more than a personal story. Through powerful reflections and relatable moments, Leela invites us to look inward and take ownership of our own path. I learned a lot, especially about myself."

Clinton Wingrove- HR Consultant

"This journey is a call to live and lead with intention. Leela blends personal truth with practical guidance, offering a rare combination of authenticity and clarity that stays with you long after you put the book down."

Collette Ijeoma- Marketing Officer

"Through powerful storytelling and human insight, Leela invites you to face your fears, push your limits, and reclaim your voice. If you have ever felt like an outsider, this book will speak directly to you."

Mohit Kanade- Strategy & Transformation Leader

BEYOND THE ICE

BEYOND THE ICE

Foreword

When I first met Leela I sensed an extraordinary strength. That sense only deepened when we shared the unforgettable experience of trekking across the Arctic Circle. In temperatures of minus 40 degrees centigrade that tested every fibre of our physical and emotional resilience, I watched Leela move not only with courage but with compassion. She listened, she cared, and she held space for others, even as the wind howled and the ground beneath us shifted, both literally and metaphorically.

Reading Beyond the Ice felt, in many ways, like walking alongside her again.

In this deeply personal and profoundly practical book, Leela weaves together the rawness of her lived experience, growing up as a brown girl in a white adoptive family, navigating trauma, and carving a path in a world that too often asked her to shrink. With leadership lessons that are urgent, transformative, and actionable, Leela shows us that the truest leaders are not those who shout the loudest but those who dare to turn inward first. And thus she has written something of a rarity - a leadership book that speaks directly to the heart of belonging.

As the CEO of an organisation committed to building inclusive, psychologically safe cultures in some of the world's largest employers, I know that belonging isn't built in boardrooms alone - it's built in the courage to show up as we are, again and again. Leela's words remind us that identity, trauma, and resilience are not side notes in the leadership story – they are the story.

This book does not offer neat answers. Instead, it asks powerful, braver questions: Who are you when the mask comes off? What does it mean to belong, not just to a place or a team, but to yourself? How can you lead in a way that remains true to who you are? And if you have the privilege of leading others, how will you show up – for everyone, and especially, for those from historically marginalised communities?

This is not just a leadership book, it is a call to conscience.

Leela's voice is both searing and generous. Leela reminds us that growth doesn't happen in the comfort zone. It happens when we lose our footing, fumble for warmth, face our biases, and, in the words of Maggie Khun, who also challenged biases, to speak up even when our voice shakes. Ultimately, it happens when we stop trying to fit in and start choosing to stand tall.

The Women's Arctic Challenge expedition culminated in Canada, so it seems fitting to quote the lyrics of one of the nation's iconic singer-songwriters. "You live, you learn," Alanis Morissette sang. "You lose, you learn / You cry, you learn / You bleed, you learn." Leela has done all of this and more. But what elevates this book beyond memoir or manual, is the generosity with which she shares her journey. She has taken the ice, the corporate bruises, the silences, and turned them into a roadmap. And she invites us to walk it too, with self-awareness, clarity, kindness, and trust.

To borrow once more from Morissette, "You grieve, you learn / You choke, you learn / You laugh, you learn / You choose, you learn." In Beyond the Ice, Leela doesn't just tell us this. She shows us. And in

BEYOND THE ICE

doing so, she makes space for all of us to learn, lead, and belong a little more bravely.

Hayley Barnard

CEO, MIX Diversity

BEYOND THE ICE

About the Author 17
The Eleven Core Principles 33
A roadmap for transformation 33

CHAPTER 1
Self-Awareness - understanding your impact 39

CHAPTER 2
Clarity - Finding alignment in chaos 51

CHAPTER 3
Love and Kindness - The power of small actions 67

CHAPTER 4
Resilience - Thriving through adversity 85

CHAPTER 5
Courage - Facing fear with action 109

CHAPTER 6
Trust - The fuel that powers meaningful relationships 127

CHAPTER 7
Connection - The bonds that unite us 153

CHAPTER 8
Leadership - Inspiring others through action .. 174

CHAPTER 9
Diversity - Strengthening our differences 199

CHAPTER 10
Belonging - The journey back to myself 225

CHAPTER 11

BEYOND THE ICE

Legacy - Creating impact beyond ourselves ... 253

Acknowledgements 266

My Greatest Legacy 267

Epilogue 269

Connect with Leela 272

BEYOND THE ICE

About the Author

Leela Bassi is a keynote speaker, facilitator, and founder of **Above & Beyond Resilience**, a company dedicated to building inclusive cultures, resilient leadership, and workplaces where everyone feels seen, valued, and empowered to thrive.

Born in India and raised in France, Leela's life has been shaped by the intersection of cultures, courage, and compassion. Her journey, from orphanage to boardroom, from rejection to belonging, and from silence to impact, has inspired thousands across the world.

With over twenty-five years of experience in international corporate environments, Leela now works across sectors and borders to support organisations in embracing diversity, equity, and inclusion as both a human and strategic imperative. Her work blends storytelling, neuroscience, and practical leadership tools to create lasting cultural shifts.

Leela is known for her deeply personal and powerful approach to leadership development, bringing vulnerability, humour, and honesty to every stage she steps onto. Whether she's guiding executives, mentoring young professionals, or leading conversations about bias and belonging, her message remains the same:

BEYOND THE ICE

True transformation starts when we go above and beyond, together.

She lives in Windsor in the South East of the UK, with her family, and continues to champion the belief that legacy is not what we leave behind, but how we lead while we are here.

BEYOND THE ICE

A note before we begin - One expedition, many stories

The Arctic expedition I describe in this book is deeply personal. it is told through my eyes, shaped by my experiences, emotions, and reflections. But I was not alone out there. We were a group; twelve women from different walks of life, united by a common goal but living individual stories.

We shared tents in twos (or three in my case) and cooked in groups of four. Which meant that much of what happened unfolded in pockets, small bubbles of experience that weren't always visible to everyone else. What happened in one tent might never have been seen or felt by those in another. Some mornings, if a tent packed up faster than another, they moved ahead before the others even set off. We all saw a different sky, heard different conversations, felt different emotions.

And so, while we journeyed together across that frozen landscape, we were also each walking our own path.

If you are one of the women who stood beside me on that ice, I want you to know, this is my story, not *the* story. I honour your version, even the parts I did not witness, even the things I did not know were happening at the time.

Our shared journey was a mosaic of moments, and this book offers just one piece of it. I hope it inspires others, and I hope it reminds us all, of the quiet, often unseen courage it takes to simply keep moving forward, one step at a time.

BEYOND THE ICE

To protect the privacy of the women who took part in this expedition, I have changed their names. This was done with care and respect, so each of them can retain ownership of their own story, whether shared publicly or kept quietly within.

Early Years – Finding my voice in a world of questions

I was about 10 years old, and my class was preparing for a group performance. I was excited to participate, but when roles were handed out, I was placed at the very back of the group, nearly out of sight. When I asked why, the teacher said, *"It is just how it worked out."* But deep down, I couldn't shake the feeling that my appearance played a part. Being different, I learned, sometimes meant being invisible.

Long before I understood the full story of where I came from, I knew I was different.

I was born in India, abandoned at birth by my father after my mother supposedly died, and raised by nuns in an orphanage in Bangalore. At the age of two, I was adopted by a white French family who already had three biological children. We lived in a quiet, working-class town in northern France where difference was both noticed and rarely spoken about.

School was one of the first places where I felt the weight of that difference. I was often left on the sidelines, watching the ease with which others belonged. Birthday party invitations never came. The questions came often, "Where are you from?" "No, but where are you really from?" No answer ever seemed to satisfy.

And the rejection did not end there. It came from the place where I should have felt safest. My adoptive father was physically abusive. He beat us - me more than the others. The others had learned to stay quiet. I hadn't. He was a builder who worked hard to support the family, but that did not excuse the violence. In his eyes, I needed to be taught what a "*good girl*" should be like. Maybe his own childhood, growing up in a time when emotions were rarely expressed, had hardened him.

I pushed back; loudly and often, like many teenagers would. But I was also carrying far more. Layers of grief and confusion, wounds I did not yet have the words for, and a quiet longing to be accepted without having to fight for it.

My adoptive mother was submissive, worn down by fear. When my father was not there, she tried to protect us. She stepped between us more than once and sometimes took the punches herself. But as I grew older, she had lost the strength to fight. Instead, she would quietly plead with me, "*Do not answer him, just let it go,*" whenever he was looking for trouble. She was scared of him, and over time, that fear became her silence.

Looking back now, I realise I was not just carrying the weight of childhood. I was enduring school. Bracing myself at home. Trying to exist in a world that did not yet know how to hold someone like me.

There were other betrayals, too. One of my brothers crossed the line more than once. It was never acknowledged. But like so many women who carry these hidden scars, I learned to live with it, and to keep going.

My father died in 2012. After his funeral, I cried for three whole months, not for the man he had been, but for the dad I never had. For the relationship we never shared. For the love that never came.

But my story is not about staying invisible. It is about finding my voice in a world that was not always ready to hear it.

The first person to help me see my potential was not a parent or a relative; it was one of my teachers. At seventeen, I was battling years of rejection and self-doubt. But she saw something in me I hadn't yet recognised in myself.

One day, during a conversation about my struggles, Miss C told me, "You do not need to be like everyone else to matter. Your voice matters because it is yours." Those words did not just stick with me, they sparked a shift in how I viewed myself.

With her encouragement, I began to reclaim my confidence. She challenged me to think differently about my identity, my strengths, and my place in the world. Her belief in me was a turning point that not only shaped my path but also my understanding of what it means to help others.

Incredibly, Miss C is still by my side today; not as a mentor, but as my best friend Sabine. Across countries and over decades, we've remained connected, sharing life's highs and lows. What began in a classroom became a lifelong bond.

This resilience did not stop in France. After finishing my studies, I made the bold decision to move to the UK, alone, with nothing but a suitcase and a desire to build a new life. My first job was as an au pair, a far cry from the career I'd envisioned. But I worked hard, studied again, and eventually landed my first corporate job, where I met my husband.

The UK came with a different set of challenges. Bullying, harassment, and jealousy became realities I had to face in the workplace. Once again, I had to stand my ground, just as I had in France. The lessons from my early years, resilience, adaptability, and finding my voice, proved invaluable as I stepped into this new chapter.

Those early years shaped more than just my resilience. They taught me when to fight, when to walk away, and how to read the silences in a room. That awareness became the foundation for the work I do today. Every time I coach someone to find their voice, I think of that little girl standing at the back of the group, wondering if she belonged.

That same resilience carried me all the way to the Arctic Circle decades later, where resilience took on a whole new meaning. But before I could find strength in the ice and snow, I had to learn to find it in myself, standing my ground in France, rebuilding my life in England, and discovering what it means to truly belong in a world that often seeks to exclude.

Why this book matters

"Beyond the Ice is more than a story of resilience; it is a journey of transformation. It is about courage, trust, and connection. But most of all, it is about belonging."

Why this book?

For much of my life, I felt like an outsider. I did not belong in my family, at school, or in the workplaces where I worked so hard to prove my worth. I tried to fit in, to contort myself into what others expected, to silence the parts of me that felt 'too different.' But no matter how hard I tried, I always felt like I was standing on the edge, watching, waiting, hoping for acceptance.

So, I started running. I took part in several races, both in and outside of school, and discovered I was actually quite good at it. Over time, I pushed myself further: completing triathlons, half marathons, Tough Mudder and even a Moon Walk. These challenges gave me small victories and moments of self-belief, but deep down, I was still searching for something bigger. Something that would shake me out of the roles I had been trying to play.

That is when the Arctic expedition appeared. A challenge so far beyond anything I had ever done, I knew it would either break me or completely reshape me. I was not an explorer or an endurance athlete. I was just someone who wanted to prove to herself that she could do something extraordinary. I did not know it at the time, but that journey into the ice would teach me lessons that would change the way I saw the world, and myself.

This book is about those lessons.

It is about resilience, courage, trust, leadership, and the power of human connection. It is about the invisible barriers we carry within us and the ones society places in front of us. But most of all, it is about what happens when we choose to step beyond those barriers, *beyond the ice*, into a world where we truly belong.

Who this book is for?

This book is for anyone who has ever felt like they did not have a seat at the table. For the ones who have been underestimated, dismissed, or told they did not belong. It is for those who feel stuck, waiting for the validation to step into the fullness of who they are.

Whether you're a leader striving to build trust and create spaces where people thrive because of their differences, not despite them, or part of a team going through change and uncertainty, this book offers practical tools and powerful stories to guide you.

It is also for small business owners, whether you lead a team of one or five, or work directly with clients and customers, who want to lead with authenticity and impact. If you work in a charity, a start-up, or a community-driven organisation and want to make a meaningful difference, the lessons in these pages will support your journey.

And perhaps most importantly, this book is for anyone on a personal path of growth, seeking the courage to step fully into their own power, without waiting for permission.

The ice as a metaphor

The Arctic was brutal. It was -40°C, with 80km/h winds that stole the breath from my lungs. It was a place where nothing was easy, where even the smallest mistake could cost you dearly. But it was also a place of clarity.

Out there, stripped of comfort, titles, and pretences, you see things differently. You see what truly matters.

The ice became a metaphor for the barriers we face in life. It represented the self-doubt that quietly holds us back, the fear of rejection that silences our voices, and the unconscious biases that shape our experiences in ways we do not always recognise. But *beyond the ice*, beyond the fear and the doubt, there is something more. There is courage. There is trust. There is belonging.

What I hope you take away

If there's one thing I have learned, it is that belonging begins the moment you decide to show up as your full self. You are stronger than you think. And the most powerful transformation often happens when we step outside our comfort zones, into the unfamiliar.

As you read this book, I invite you to reflect on your own journey. Think about the barriers that may have stood in your way, the fears that have kept you silent or small, and the places in your life where you long for a deeper sense of belonging. These questions aren't always easy, but reflecting on them with curiosity can open unexpected doors to growth.

Final Thought

If you're reading this, it means something inside you is seeking change. You are exactly where you are meant to be. This book is not just my story; it is a call to step into your own story.

So, let's begin. Let's step beyond the ice together.

The Framework: Eleven Core Principles for Growth and Impact

Every journey of transformation, whether personal, professional, or within a team, relies on core principles that guide us through challenges, shape our resilience, and enable us to create a meaningful impact. This book is not just about my journey through the Arctic or my personal struggles with identity and belonging, it is about what those experiences taught me, insights that can help you traverse your own path. That's why I call them *core principles*, they are not surface-level techniques, but foundations shaped by lived experience.

These core principles emerged from extreme environments, workplace boardrooms, and deeply personal reflections. They are the shared elements that connect endurance in polar temperatures to leading high-performing teams and overcoming exclusion to build a true sense of belonging.

Each chapter explores one of these core principles in depth, offering stories, insights, and actionable strategies to apply them in your life and work.

While these principles may not reflect every one of my personal values, (such as honesty, integrity and humility) they are still deeply connected to the way I try to live those values every day.

These core principles are more than strategies for growth. They are reflections of what I believe matters most in the moments that shape us. They did not come from textbooks, but from discomfort, challenge, and deep reflection. That is why they sit at the heart of this book.

BEYOND THE ICE

ABOVE & BEYOND RESILIENCE — 11 KEY PRINCIPLES

1. Self Awareness — Understanding your impact

2. Clarity — Finding alignment in chaos

3. Love & Kindness — The power of small actions

4. Resilience — Thriving through adversity

5. Courage — Facing fear with action

6. Trust — The fuel that powers meaningful relationships

7. Connection — The bonds that unite us

8. Leadership — Inspiring others through action

9. Diversity — Strength in our differences

10. Belonging — The journey back to ourselves

11. Legacy — Creating impact beyond ourselves

BEYOND THE ICE

The Eleven Core Principles

A roadmap for transformation

1.Self-Awareness: Understanding your impact
Before we can lead others, we must first understand ourselves. Self-awareness is not just about recognising strengths and weaknesses, but about understanding the impact of our words, actions, and influence on those around us.

2.Clarity: Finding alignment in chaos
Clarity is not about knowing every step of the journey, it is about defining your direction. In a world full of distractions and competing priorities, clarity helps cut through the noise and focus on what truly matters. It transforms overwhelming challenges into actionable steps, ensuring that our energy is spent moving forward, not spinning in circles. Whether in leadership, decision-making, or personal growth, clarity keeps us aligned with our values and purpose.

3.Love & Kindness: The power of small actions
Kindness is often dismissed as a 'soft skill', but it is one of the most powerful forces for connection and change. The smallest acts - a listening ear, a moment of encouragement - can transform relationships, teams, and even our own self-belief.

4. Resilience: Thriving through adversity

True resilience is not about pushing through at all costs, but about managing energy, knowing when to rest, and understanding how to adapt in the face of setbacks.

5. Courage: Facing fear with action

Fear is a constant companion in life. Whether it is stepping outside our comfort zone, speaking up in a difficult conversation, or taking a leap into the unknown, courage is not the absence of fear, but the decision to act despite it.

6. Trust: The fuel that powers meaningful relationships

Trust is built in small, consistent moments and extraordinary acts. It requires both the courage to express ourselves and the humility to listen. Whether in extreme conditions or everyday interactions, trust is the bond that keeps people united.

7. Connection: The bonds that unite us

At our core, we all seek connection; to be seen, heard, and valued. The stories we share, the empathy we cultivate, and the relationships we nurture, define the richness of our lives.

8. Leadership: Inspiring others through action

Leadership is not about titles or authority, but about how we show up for others. True leadership is about creating an environment where people feel empowered, included, and able to thrive.

9. *Diversity: Strengthening our differences*
Diversity is not just about representation; it is about removing barriers and unlocking potential. Different perspectives lead to better decisions, stronger teams, and more innovative solutions, but only when diversity is valued and acted upon.

10. *Belonging: The journey back to ourselves*
Belonging is not about fitting in; it is about embracing who we truly are and creating spaces where others feel safe to do the same. Whether in families, teams, or organisations, true belonging transforms how we show up in the world.

11. *Legacy: Creating impact beyond ourselves*
What we do matters, but the impact we leave behind is what truly defines us. Our actions, words, and choices ripple outward, shaping lives, industries, and futures in ways we may never fully see.

How to use this book

Each chapter will explore one of these eleven core principles, weaving together personal stories, lessons from the Arctic and the corporate world, and practical strategies to help you apply these insights in your own life.

At the end of each chapter, you will find:

☑ Reflection Prompts to deepen your understanding and explore how the themes relate to your own life.
☑ Calls to Action to help you apply the insights in practical, real-world ways.
☑ Final Thoughts to reinforce the core message and leave you with a lasting takeaway.

This is not just a book to read, it is a book to experience. By engaging with these core principles, you will gain tools to build resilience, lead with impact, and create a deeper sense of belonging in your own life and work.

At the end of each chapter, there is a space for you to make notes, to set your intentions, and record your thoughts and actions.

Why do these core principles matter now?

The world is constantly changing, and uncertainty is inevitable. Whether you are leading a team, handling personal challenges, or striving for personal growth, these core principles will help you adapt, connect, and create lasting impact.

This book is for anyone who wants to lead with purpose, embrace challenges with courage, and build meaningful relationships, both at work and in life, and within themselves.

Alongside this book, I have created a companion journal called *"Beyond the ice: Reset, Rise and Repeat"*, designed to help you pause, reflect, and take action. It includes prompts, exercises, and space to explore your own journey as you read. Whether you are working through personal growth, leadership challenges, or simply want a place to reflect, the journal is there to support you. You can use it chapter by chapter or come back to it at the end.

Your journey starts here.

BEYOND THE ICE

CHAPTER 1

Self-Awareness - understanding your impact

"When I discover who I am, I will be free."
Ralph Ellison

In this chapter, we begin with one of the most powerful and sometimes confronting aspects of growth: self-awareness. It is not just about how well you know yourself, but also about how clearly you understand how others experience you. There are two levels to this: the internal world, where you interpret your values, emotions, and motivations, and the external view, which reflects how you come across to others. Often, the gap between these two can shape your success or quietly hold you back.

We will explore how blind spots, (those unnoticed patterns or behaviours), can limit our impact without us even realising. These blind spots are rarely intentional, but when they go unexamined, they can block connection, erode trust, and prevent us from becoming the leader or person we truly want to be.

But insight alone is not enough. Self-awareness is only meaningful when it drives action. Knowing yourself matters, but what you choose to do with that knowledge matters more. In this chapter, we will explore how to translate self-awareness into meaningful change, and how taking responsibility for your own patterns can unlock real growth.

Seeing yourself clearly

It was the first day back at school after half term. I must have been in lower school. That day, we had a substitute teacher. As she read through the register, she paused. Her brow furrowed when she reached my name.

"Leila?" she said tentatively. "No, it is Leela," I corrected. She tried again. "Lila?" I shook my head. "Leela," I repeated softly.

She looked up from the paper, clearly unsure. "What nationality are you?" "French," I replied. She gave a tight smile. "*You know what I mean.*" "No, I don't," I said quietly.

The class was silent. Her tone was not aggressive, but it cut through me. In that moment, something shifted. I had always felt French, until someone saw me and decided I did not look the part. I was not struggling with my name. (Everyone else was). But somehow, I was the one made to feel like I did not belong.

That moment made me realise that just when you think you have found ease in who you are, someone's assumptions can pull the ground from under you. At its core, self-awareness is not just about how you see yourself. It is just as much about how others perceive and respond to you.

More than just reflection

Self-awareness is often mistaken for simply *knowing yourself*, your likes, dislikes, strengths, and weaknesses. But true self-awareness goes beyond introspection. It is about understanding how you show up in the world, how others experience you, and how your actions impact those around you.

Many of us go through life unaware of the subconscious patterns that drive our decisions. We think we know why we react a certain way, but often, we are operating on autopilot, shaped by past experiences, cultural conditioning, and blind spots we've never questioned.

BEYOND THE ICE

The Arctic - When self-awareness was survival

In extreme conditions, self-awareness is not just useful, it is essential. In the Arctic, a lack of awareness about your own body, mindset, or impact on others could mean the difference between life and death.

One morning, I woke up struggling to move my fingers. The temperatures had plummeted overnight, and my body had not fully adjusted. I had underestimated how tightly I needed to secure my gloves, and the cold had seeped through, leaving my hands numb. I thought I was fine... until I was not.

What I have come to understand about self-awareness is that we often think we are fine until something forces us to confront the truth.

But self-awareness in the Arctic, was not just about monitoring our own well-being; it was also about reading each other. Out there, no one had the luxury of stubbornness or pride. We had to be honest about our limitations and alert to the unspoken struggles of others.

One night, while setting up camp, I noticed that Eden was moving slower than usual, her face expressionless. She was usually full of energy, always the first to crack a joke. But tonight, she was silent.

I hesitated. Was she just tired, or was something wrong?

I had two choices: ignore it and hope she was fine, or check in. I chose the latter.

"Hey, how are you holding up?" I asked gently.

She exhaled deeply before admitting, *"Honestly? I can't feel my toes, and I did not want to make a fuss."*

That moment reminded me that self-awareness is not just about ourselves, it is also about noticing others. By the time frostbite sets in, it is often too late. In fact, ten years later, Eden still has permanent nerve damage and hasn't felt her toes since that expedition. A lasting reminder of how pain can be silent, and how vital it is to check in.

Internal vs external self-awareness

Research by Tasha Eurich, an organisational psychologist, highlights two types of self-awareness:

1. Internal self-awareness – the extent to which you understand yourself, your values, strengths, weaknesses, and emotions.
2. External self-awareness – how well you understand how others perceive you.

Most people assume they are self-aware, but studies show that only about 10-15% of people actually are.

You may believe you're a great listener, but do others feel truly heard by you? You may think you handle pressure well, but do your colleagues experience you as calm, or as someone who unknowingly spreads stress?

The gap between how we see ourselves and how others experience us can be eye-opening. And sometimes, it takes an unexpected moment to realise the truth.

Workplace - When feedback became a mirror

I used to believe I was a good communicator: clear, direct, and efficient. But early in my career, I received feedback that made me pause: "*You sometimes come across as too sharp. People hesitate to approach you because they're unsure how you will react.*" At first, I was defensive. "*I am just being direct,* is not that a strength?"

But when I reflected, I realised something deeper: how I saw myself was not always how others experienced me. I was not intentionally being cold, but my focus on efficiency sometimes made people feel as though they were being dismissed.

Would this same feedback have been given to someone else in the same way? When a white male colleague spoke directly, he was seen as assertive or a natural leader. When I did the same, as a woman of colour, it was labelled as sharp or intimidating.

This doesn't only apply to women of colour. Many women, regardless of their background, are told they're too direct, too assertive, too emotional, as if their confidence or clarity needs to be toned down to make others comfortable. But for women of colour, those labels can carry an additional weight, shaped by both gendered and racial bias.

The truth is that people tend to assign labels quickly when they do not know you. A white male colleague might be seen as having a valid reason for being upset: "*Oh, he's frustrated because he has a lot on his plate.*" But a woman, particularly a woman of colour, might be described as "emotional," "intimidating," or "hard to work with." The same behaviour, different interpretations.

This strength: our directness, our presence, reminds us that daring to speak, daring to fight, or even to exist in a system not designed for us is an act of resistance in itself.

This made me think more deeply about how bias affects perception, and how those perceptions shape our ability to influence. I did not want to change who I was, but I did want to ensure that my intentions and my impact were aligned. Instead of expecting others to interpret my directness in the right way, I made small but significant adjustments. I replaced the interrogative "why" with the inclusive "why," knowing that, "Why did you do this?" could sound like a challenge, while, *"Can you walk me through your thinking?"* created openness. I asked more questions before offering solutions and shared my perspective. I also created space for connection before diving into tasks, making sure to begin with people, not just the work.

And guess what? My impact improved. I was still clear, direct, and efficient, but now I was also being received the way I intended to be.

Lesson: Self-awareness is not just about knowing who you are, it is about recognising how others experience you. The gap between intention and impact can hold us back, especially when bias is at play. But when we approach this with honesty and courage, we begin to close that gap and influence others, not by changing who we are, but by showing up more intentionally as who we *truly* are.

Over the years, I have realised that there are parts of myself I see clearly, and others I have only discovered through the eyes of others. Sometimes it is a strength I have overlooked, or a habit I did not know I had, like interrupting or rushing when I am nervous. These aren't flaws. They're just patterns. And the more I have been willing to ask for feedback or sit with uncomfortable moments, the more I have grown.

We all have blind spots. Not because we're unaware, but because we're human. True self-awareness means staying curious about ourselves. It means being open to the idea that how we think we show up might not be how others experience us. Instead of seeing that as criticism, we can see it as a gift, a chance to align our intention with our impact.

Self-awareness in action - Practical tools for growth

So how do we build this kind of awareness in real life?

Start by inviting honest feedback from people who see you in different contexts. Choose three individuals, one from your workplace, one from your personal life, and one from a community or social setting, and ask them two questions:

"What's one strength I bring to our relationship?"

And...

"What's one thing I do that might unintentionally hold me back?"

The key is to listen without defending. Just absorb. What you hear might surprise you, or it might affirm what you already suspected.

You can also begin a simple, daily check-in with yourself. At the end of the day, ask: What moment made me feel most like myself today? When did I feel off balance or reactive? What might have triggered that response? And how might my energy or behaviour have impacted someone else? Over time, these reflections begin to reveal patterns, and patterns create the opportunity for change.

Another powerful practice is pausing when you feel emotionally triggered. Rather than reacting on autopilot, take a breath and name the emotion. Say to yourself, "I feel dismissed," rather than simply thinking, "I am angry." Then ask, "What do I need right now?" or "Is this the right moment to respond?" This moment of mindfulness helps you choose your response instead of being driven by it.

Finally, if you hear the same feedback from different people like, "You often interrupt" or "You shut down when stressed", pay attention. Repeated feedback is rarely random. It is often a doorway to deeper insight. Once acknowledged, those blind spots can become breakthroughs.

Reflection Prompt

Which of these tools feels most relevant to your life right now? What would it look like to try it for the next 7 days?

Call to Action

Pick one moment this week to pause and ask yourself, "How am I showing up right now?" Then act from awareness, not autopilot. Because when you act from awareness, you do not just grow, you leave a more intentional mark on the people and world around you.

Final Thought

Self-awareness is not a fixed trait; it is a daily choice. A quiet strength that grows each time we pause, reflect, and adjust with intention. When we close the gap between how we think we show up and how others experience us, we do not just build trust, we become the kind of person, teammate, or leader others feel safe to grow alongside.

And for those of us navigating systems that were not built with us in mind, choosing to speak up, to take space, and to lead with clarity is not just self-awareness, it is a quiet act of resistance.

… BEYOND THE ICE

Notes

BEYOND THE ICE

CHAPTER 2

Clarity - Finding alignment in chaos

"He who has a why to live can bear almost any how." - Friedrich Nietzsche

This chapter is about that voice. The inner critic. The one that whispers, "You're not enough." The one that almost stopped me from going to the Arctic.

In this chapter, we will explore how clarity helps us cut through chaos and focus on what truly matters. It is easy to assume that clarity comes from knowing every step in advance, but more often, it is about staying grounded when the path ahead is uncertain.

In the Arctic, even the smallest miscommunication could lead to major consequences: frozen supplies, unsafe conditions, or hours lost retracing our steps. In the workplace, it shows up as missed deadlines, misunderstood expectations, or burnout. And in life, clarity is what helps us move forward when everything feels overwhelming.

We will explore what happens when plans change suddenly, when assumptions replace instructions, and when values get buried beneath urgency. Through stories from the Arctic, from teams I have worked with, and from my own experience starting over in a new country, we will see how clarity is not about perfection. It is about taking the next step with intention, and knowing what matters most, even when the future is still foggy.

The power of clarity - Turning uncertainty into opportunity

In a world filled with distractions, constant demands, and competing priorities, clarity can feel like a luxury. Yet, it is the foundation for everything we do. Without clarity, we waste time, energy, and resources. We spin in circles, unsure of where to go or how to start. But with clarity, even the most daunting challenges become manageable.

Take, for example, a moment when a client requested something entirely new, something outside our comfort zone. At first, it felt overwhelming. But when we stepped back, visualised success, and broke the task into clear steps, the path forward began to reveal itself. Clarity is not about eliminating complexity. It is about cutting through the noise to focus on what truly matters.

BEYOND THE ICE

Arctic - When clarity gets tested and redefined

In the Arctic, clarity was not optional; it was the difference between progress and setback, between safety and risk.

If I did not know how much water I'd drunk or where I'd packed my dry gloves, I paid the price quickly. I learned to prepare intentionally, strip back the unnecessary, and stay focused on the essentials. Each day, we had to decide on our route, align our actions, and move forward as a team. There was no room for ambiguity. A wrong turn or a poorly communicated plan could mean hours lost, energy wasted, or even life-threatening consequences.

On our first day, visibility was low, the wind was howling, and the cold bit through every layer of clothing. Then, just hours into our trek, my tent buddy Sally dislocated her ankle. At first, we thought she might recover with rest, but as we continued, it became clear she couldn't go on. We had no choice but to stop. Everything had to be reassessed and reclarified. Our route changed. Roles shifted. The plan we had set that morning was no longer relevant. The clarity we thought we had was shattered, and we had to pause and find a new plan together.

While we refocused on our purpose and realigned as a team, I couldn't help but think about Sally. The impact was profound. Her dream of completing the expedition was shattered within minutes. All the preparation, the training, and the mental resilience she had built up came to an abrupt halt. I will never forget the moment she was told she'd need to return to base and wait for us to complete the journey. Watching her process the news was heart-wrenching.

That is when it hit us: it could have been any of us. Clarity is not always about rigidly sticking to a plan. It is about having the awareness and courage to pause, reassess, and respond to what is actually happening.

Lesson: Sometimes, clarity is not about the plan ahead but about embracing where you are right now, even when it is not where you hoped to be.

Arctic - The frozen toothpaste lesson

Our first night in the Arctic, we received clear instructions: "Keep your essentials in your sleeping bag so they do not freeze overnight."

After hours of trekking in icy conditions, all we wanted was to climb into our sleeping bags to get warm. Exhausted, we tossed lip balm, pots of cream, and deodorant to the bottom of the bag, gave it a good shake for luck, and hoped for the best.

By morning, we discovered everything was rock solid. The cold had seeped through, and we found ourselves tackling frozen toothpaste in temperatures well below zero. The real instruction had been to keep items close to our bodies, where body heat would prevent them from freezing. A slight miscommunication led to a frustrating mistake. It was not intentional, but the consequences were immediate.

Lesson: Clarity is not just about giving instructions. It is about ensuring they're understood the way you intended.

This principle shows up just as often in everyday environments, especially at work.

Workplace - Misalignment and missed goals

In one organisation I worked with, a manager tasked the team with *"improving customer satisfaction."* It sounded straightforward, but each member interpreted it differently. One team member focused on speeding up response times. Another redesigned the feedback form. Others weren't sure where to start. The result? Overlapping efforts, wasted energy, and no meaningful progress.

The same principle applies at home. I recall an instance when I asked my daughter to "tidy her room." I expected it to include folding clothes and putting books on the shelf, but her interpretation was shoving everything under the bed. To her, the room looked tidy. To me, it was anything but.

Lesson: Misalignment is not always about bad intent. It is about different assumptions.

Personal story - The misaligned school project

I vividly recall a moment from school when my teacher asked us to complete a 'creative project' over the weekend. Excited, I spent hours drawing and colouring a detailed poster, only to find out on Monday that the assignment required a written essay.

I was crushed. All that effort, and I'd missed the point. The same pattern followed me into adulthood: misunderstanding instructions, missing expectations, feeling like I'd failed, when all I lacked was clarity.

BEYOND THE ICE

Lesson: Clarity is not just about instruction. It is about shared understanding.

This theme of shared understanding became even more critical when facing physically and mentally demanding environments.

BEYOND THE ICE

Arctic - Breaking down big goals

Standing at the start of a 100-kilometre Arctic trek was overwhelming. The cold was biting, the distance ahead stretched endlessly, and the weight of what lay before us pressed hard on everyone's shoulders.

The sheer scale of the challenge could have been paralysing. But instead of thinking about the whole journey, we broke it down. One day at a time. Ten kilometres. One foot in front of the other.

The plan was simple: complete that day's trek, then focus on the next. No fixating on the finish line. No spinning into "*what ifs?*" Just stay present and take the next right step.

Before we knew it, the milestones added up. Suddenly, the once intimidating finish line felt within reach. Breaking the journey into smaller, measurable chunks did not just make it manageable it also kept us motivated. Every step was intentional. Every decision deliberate.

Because in those conditions, the journey depended on it. That mindset of focusing on the next right step did not just get us through the Arctic. It became just as essential in fast-moving, high-pressure environments of corporate life.

Workplace and personal clarity in crisis

I once worked with a team trying to rebuild trust with a frustrated client. The situation felt messy. But when we stopped to clarify priorities, everything changed. We focused on three steps: address the pain point, offer a quick win, then build a longer-term plan. That approach did not just repair trust; it strengthened the partnership.

This step-by-step mindset became my personal compass as well. When I moved to the UK, everything felt uncertain. I had no roadmap. I just knew I needed to start. First: find a job. Then: save for education. Finally, build a network. One step at a time.

That same step-by-step mindset has carried me through some of the biggest adventures of my life.

In 2015, I crossed the Arctic with a team of extraordinary women. In 2019, I returned to India to reconnect with my roots, a journey I will share later in Chapter 10.

Now, looking ahead to 2025, I felt the call for another challenge. Another moment that would stretch me, humble me, and remind me what I am capable of: that is why I decided to trek to Everest Base Camp. This decision did not come from nowhere; it was the next chapter in a journey defined by intentional steps. Some might say it is crazy, but for me, this feels like a natural continuation of the journey I started long ago. A way of honouring the instinct to keep stepping beyond my comfort zone, to keep testing my edges, and to keep discovering new versions of myself along the way. Just like every time before, I know that reaching a distant goal is not about giant leaps. It is about focusing on the very next step.

So I began preparing the only way I knew how: one step at a time.

Cardio to build endurance. Resistance training for power. Breathwork to prepare for altitude. Hydration to prevent fatigue. Each small action matters, and together they form the foundation for a 150-kilometre journey across extreme terrain. It is not the destination alone that defines the experience. It is the disciplined preparation, the clarity of intention, and the decision to keep moving, even when the goal still feels far away. And just like every journey before, it reminds me: clarity is not about having all the answers. It is about knowing the next right step and trusting yourself to take it.

Lesson: Clarity transforms overwhelming goals into achievable actions.

In my own life, what sustained me through uncertainty was not just setting goals. It was anchoring to clear values, hence I chose resilience, curiosity, and integrity as my guideposts. Whether I was rebuilding from scratch, balancing two cultures, or training for Everest, clarity came from alignment.

Personal - Values as a compass

When I moved to the UK, my goal was to build a better life. But what sustained me was clarity of values.

I leaned into resilience, refusing to let setbacks define me. I nurtured my curiosity, seeing every challenge as a learning opportunity. And I held onto persistence, knowing that giving up was never an option.

Balancing my French upbringing with my Indian identity was not easy. Growing up as an adopted Indian child in a white French family, I often felt unsure of where I belonged. Was I meant to assimilate fully into French culture, or connect with an Indian identity I had never truly known?

Eventually, I realised that clarity was not about choosing one identity over the other. It was about defining my own values. Resilience. Curiosity. Integrity. Those became my compass, guiding me in every environment. Even small things, like hearing "loo" instead of "water closet," reminded me that clarity was not just about language. It was about learning new expectations and adapting, without losing who I was.

Lesson: Defining your values gives you the clarity to adapt without losing who you are.

The Arctic test - When alignment was key

In the Arctic, aligning our values with our actions was a matter of life and death.

After a long, exhausting day of trekking, one of our leaders prepared tomato soup to lift our spirits. But by the time it reached us, it was more like gazpacho. It was cold and unappetising, and far from the comforting warmth we had imagined. Disheartened, a few of us left it outside the tent.

By morning, the soup had frozen solid. More importantly, we received a harsh wake-up call: we had broken Arctic protocol. It could have attracted polar bears, putting the entire team at risk.

That moment made one thing clear: small, seemingly insignificant actions can have major consequences. From that point forward, we became hyper-aware of every decision, ensuring our actions aligned with the values that would keep us safe: accountability, teamwork, and discipline.

Lesson: When values and actions do not match, confusion, frustration, and risk follow.

BEYOND THE ICE

The Arctic lesson - When plans change

In the Arctic, clarity was not just about knowing the plan; it was about adapting to reality when things did not go as planned.

Whenever I lead a team or work on a project, I now take the time to ask, "What does success look like for you?" or "How do you interpret this task?" That small effort to align understanding upfront can save significant time and energy later.

I have seen how this approach transforms teams. In one organisation I worked with, we identified quarterly goals that had previously confused, missed deadlines, and duplicated efforts. By facilitating a session to define clear objectives, the team not only streamlined their actions but also achieved progress that had previously seemed out of reach.

This highlights the power of clarity: it is not just about efficiency; it is about unlocking potential. This experience not only reinforced the importance of staying calm under pressure but also taught me the value of leading with clarity and purpose, even in challenging situations.

Reflection Prompt

Think of a time when things felt uncertain or overwhelming. What gave you clarity in that moment? Now consider where you might need that same clarity in your life today. What is one value or intention that could help you take the next right step?

Call to Action

Bringing clarity into your life

Start by defining your destination. What are your top three priorities this week? Break a large goal into smaller steps. What is one clear action you can take today?

And check in with your values. Are your actions aligned with what matters most?

Because when you have clarity, everything else begins to fall into place.

Final Thought

Clarity does not require certainty. It invites us to pause, reflect, and choose the next right step, even when the full picture remains unclear. When we lead from alignment, with our values as our compass, we do not just move forward. We move with purpose.

Notes

BEYOND THE ICE

CHAPTER 3

Love and Kindness - The power of small actions

"Kindness is a language which the deaf can hear and the blind can see." - Mark Twain

In this chapter, we will explore the quiet strength of kindness, especially in moments when it might seem least expected. During the harsh and unrelenting conditions of the Arctic, it was not grand gestures that kept us going, but small, often unnoticed acts of kindness. A shared snack, a hand on the shoulder, or a few words of encouragement in a biting wind. These gestures held us together when everything else seemed to be falling apart.

Kindness is often underestimated in leadership, yet it is one of the most powerful tools we have. It cultivates psychological safety, builds trust, and allows teams to perform at their best. Through stories from extreme environments and the workplace, we will see how kindness creates space for courage and connection, not weakness or compromise.

On a more personal level, I'll share a story that challenged my assumptions about kindness and love. It is a story layered with contradiction, discomfort, and transformation. It reminded me that kindness is not always soft or easy, but it is always powerful. Sometimes, it is the very thing that helps us redefine what love means altogether.

Love, kindness and compassion - The subtle differences

Love and kindness are often seen as one and the same, but they are distinct forces. Kindness is a conscious act, something we do intentionally. Love is often quieter, deeper, and sometimes unspoken. Compassion bridges the two: the ability to recognise someone's suffering and act with warmth and understanding, without judgement.

Through the stories in this chapter, from the biting cold of the Arctic to the warmth of my Italian family, you will see how these three forces shaped my experiences. For me, they arrived over time, each helping me redefine the other.

Why love and kindness matter

Love and kindness are the invisible threads that weave together the fabric of human connection. They offer strength in vulnerability and forge bonds in moments of need. In a world often marked by division and competition, love and kindness remind us of what truly matters; the humanity we share and the connections we build.

In our fast-paced world, kindness can feel like a luxury, something reserved for when time allows. Yet, small acts of empathy and connection have the power to transform lives, strengthen teams, and build resilience in both the giver and the receiver. Kindness

BEYOND THE ICE

is not just a soft skill; it is a force that shapes leadership, deepens relationships, and sustains us through challenges.

But kindness is not about elaborate gestures. It is about empathy, noticing others' needs, and acting without expecting anything in return. Whether in the Arctic's extreme conditions, the business world, or personal relationships, kindness is the invisible bond that makes people feel seen and valued.

BEYOND THE ICE

The Arctic - A cup of warmth in the cold

The Arctic is a merciless place where survival depends on individual resilience and the collective strength of the team. In minus 40°C conditions, kindness was not optional, it was essential. A lack of kindness was not just unpleasant, it was potentially dangerous. The intense cold, piercing winds, and exhausting treks pushed us to our limits, making every moment a challenge.

Yet, in the midst of that harsh landscape, it was small acts of kindness that made all the difference. A colleague's supportive hand, a simple word of encouragement, or a shared moment of warmth became beacons, reminding us that even in the most extreme conditions, our humanity remained intact.

In the Arctic, where communication was nearly impossible due to howling gales, gestures became our language of care. Sometimes, kindness meant guiding a sled for someone struggling, helping with gear adjustments, or offering a warm drink in silence. These weren't just practical acts, they were reminders that we weren't alone.

The glove story - A small action, a big impact

One bone-chilling afternoon, I stopped to adjust my layers. Managing body temperature was crucial, sweating too much could be just as dangerous as getting too cold. In that moment, a fierce gust of wind swept one of my gloves away, sending it tumbling across the snow.

BEYOND THE ICE

Panic surged through me. My fingers were already numb, and losing a glove in the Arctic was not just inconvenient, it was a serious risk. Frostbite could set in within minutes, leading to severe damage or even the loss of a hand. Exhausted and overwhelmed, I dropped to my knees, fighting back tears.

Before I could process what was happening, my colleague Cathy sprang into action. Without hesitation, she dashed across the ice, chasing my glove through the howling wind. She plunged into the snow, caught it just before it disappeared into the white expanse, and returned, breathless but smiling.

When Cathy returned with my glove, I did not just feel relief, I felt profound gratitude and connection. In that moment, I realised that kindness is not just about helping, it is about uplifting and inspiring. In the Arctic, where every action could mean the difference between keeping my fingers or losing them, she did not wait for thanks or pause to consider her own comfort; she just acted.

Cathy's actions embodied the purest form of kindness: seeing a need and responding, without expectation of recognition or reward. That small gesture did not just save my hand; it reinforced the quiet but powerful commitment within the team to always look out for one another.

Kindness, especially in extreme conditions, doesn't just sustain morale, it reminds us of our shared humanity. True kindness doesn't emerge when things are comfortable; it appears when life is hard, when helping costs us something.

Gratitude around the table

Around the dinner table in my family, we practice nightly reflections, sharing three moments of gratitude and one act of kindness from the day. It is a small ritual but one that has shaped how we view the world. Kindness, we've learned, is a habit; a way of seeing and appreciating life's smallest moments.

In the Arctic, gratitude took on a different form. In a fierce landscape where every moment counted, even the smallest gestures carried immense significance. At the end of each exhausting day, we would acknowledge the moments that made a difference; someone extending a helping hand, a shared laugh that lightened the burden of the cold, a sip of lukewarm tea that felt like a luxury in the vast, frozen wilderness. These moments of reflection were more than words; they were anchors that kept us grounded in something beyond the struggle.

Coming home after weeks in the Arctic was a shock to the system. I will never forget the feeling of sitting on a chair at the dinner table, something so simple, yet it felt like a privilege. After weeks of crouching in snow, eating whatever we could carry close enough to stay edible, the ability to sit comfortably, without feeling the cold seep through every layer, was astonishing.

The smallest conveniences felt miraculous: being able to turn on a tap and have hot water flow instantly, using a kettle instead of melting ice over a tiny stove just to enjoy a warm drink, or stepping into a bathroom with a real toilet rather than digging a hole in the snow. These were things I had never truly appreciated until I returned.

BEYOND THE ICE

In the Arctic, every meal was a mission. Lunchtime was not a break; it was simply a practical refuelling stop in sub-zero temperatures; nothing exciting, just frozen bagels with tuna, slowly thawing against our bodies as we walked. There was no steaming plate of food waiting at the end of the day. If you weren't fast enough to grab your cutlery, (still carrying the faint taste of soap from the night before) the food cooked on the stove would freeze within seconds. There were no second helpings. No choice of meals. No complaints about preference, just gratitude for whatever we had.

Returning home, I saw everything with fresh eyes. I realised how much we take for granted, not just material comforts, but the ability to share a meal in warmth, to drink tea without rationing our supplies, to have a moment of stillness without battling the elements.

These lessons remained with me, and as a family, we continued to nurture gratitude, but our tradition evolved.

Since my son left for university, our weekly reflections evolved, alongside sharing moments of gratitude and kindness, we've added something new:

Each week, in our family group chat, we share a snapshot of our lives: a photo of something that caught our attention or brought us joy. It could be anything, such as: a song that lingered in our minds, a quote that inspired us, a poem that resonated, or even a meme that made us laugh. More than just updates, these moments are glimpses into each other's worlds, small but meaningful ways to stay connected, no matter the distance.

This practice has become a bond that binds us. Gratitude is no longer just about what we have, it is about how we experience the world, and the moments we choose to hold onto.

In the Arctic, gratitude kept us grounded. At home, it keeps us connected. And in life, it transforms ordinary days into something deeply meaningful.

Kindness, of course, extends beyond family and survival settings. It is just as vital in the boardroom, where pressure and performance often leave little room for empathy.

Kindness in leadership - Beyond being 'nice'

In the workplace, kindness is often overlooked. Some see it as a weakness, as though being kind means avoiding difficult conversations or lowering expectations. But true kindness is not about avoiding accountability: it is about leading with empathy, clarity, and intention.

Leading with empathy without losing accountability

Leading with empathy doesn't mean losing accountability. In fact, the opposite is true. When kindness is present, trust naturally grows. And when trust grows, people feel safe enough to speak up. That safety allows innovation to thrive, because people are no longer afraid to contribute or take thoughtful risks.

Workplace - Leading with kindness under pressure

During a 12-week leadership programme I facilitated, participants shared that psychological safety was the most transformative part. One leader said, "*For the first time, I felt seen, not just as an employee, but as a person with strengths, struggles, and a real voice in the room.*"

That moment reaffirmed what I already knew: kindness in leadership is not about lowering standards, it is about creating spaces where people can thrive.

And when leaders create those spaces, something powerful happens. Teams become more connected. Performance improves. People are more willing to take risks, share ideas, and support each other. Kindness is more than a feel-good concept, it drives results. Teams that lead with kindness perform better, innovate more, and experience less turnover.

A leader who notices a struggling team member and asks, "How can I support you?" sends a powerful message: You are valued. You are not alone. These moments of kindness build trust, strengthen resilience, and encourage people to bring their best selves to work. But kindness doesn't always look the same. Sometimes, what is meant as love or care can feel very different depending on how it is expressed.

Kindness also creates an environment where people feel safe to share ideas and take risks, both of which are essential for innovation. In diverse teams, kindness ensures every voice is heard, unlocking creativity that might otherwise remain hidden.

A kind leader recognises potential where others see obstacles, shaping a culture of possibility. They create spaces where people feel valued, empowered, and motivated, not just to show up, but to thrive.

Control disguised as kindness - My French family

Kindness took on a complicated meaning in my life. My adoptive parents brought me into their home as an act of kindness, giving me opportunities I might never have had. But kindness was not always reflected in my father's actions. In his mind, he believed discipline was the ultimate kindness – that tough love would prepare me for life's challenges.

While his intentions may have been well-meaning, his methods often left me feeling invisible and unloved.

Looking back, I realise those experiences shaped me in ways I never expected. They taught me that kindness is not measured by intent, but by impact. My father believed his actions were rooted in care, yet they often left me questioning my worth. It took me years to understand that true kindness is not just about what we mean to do, it is about how it makes others feel.

It was only later, through meeting my husband and his family, that I began to understand what love with no conditions truly looked like.

Unconditional love and kindness in its purest form - My Italian family

Meeting my husband was one of the best things that ever happened to me. His quiet strength, grounded patience, and generous spirit opened my eyes to a kind of love and support I'd never known before. But the real revelation came when I stepped into his family. From the moment I met his parents, I was embraced not as a guest, but as a daughter, without hesitation, without conditions. That is when I stopped calling them my "in-laws." To me, they became simply Mamma and Papa, not by obligation, but by the love they offered so freely.

This love was not loud or flashy; it was in the everyday acts that made me feel safe, seen, and truly valued. Mamma's kindness was not just in the meals she cooked, but in the way her kitchen became a place where everyone was welcome. From lasagna to risotto, her home-cooked meals were not just food, they were a symbol of belonging, of being cared for in the most genuine way. Her love was in the small gestures; a warm embrace, a soft word, and a listening ear that made you feel understood.

Papa became the father I had longed for. We can talk for hours about life, our dreams, and what truly matters. His wisdom often reminds me of Roberto Alajmo's idea that happiness is not just about being happy, it is about realising that you're happy while it is happening. I have come to understand this truth more deeply through my own family. By being present and appreciating the moments of joy, I am learning to live more fully in the now, to notice and truly embrace happiness in its simplest forms.

Through Mamma and Papa, I have learned that kindness is not a weakness. it is a quiet, powerful force that allows us to stand taller and believe in ourselves. it is about showing up for each other in both big and small ways, whether through a thoughtful conversation, a shared meal, or simply being there when needed. The love and acceptance they've given me has shaped my understanding of true strength. It is not about major actions, but about the daily acts of care, support, and patience that create a bond stronger than any words could express.

Their home became my sanctuary, not because of what was said, but because of the way I *felt* there. With them, I experienced the profound power of a love that is unconditional and free from expectation. And this is the lesson I carry with me: that true kindness strengthens us all. It lifts us up, helps us grow, and empowers us to show up for others in the same way.

Through my Italian family, I have learned that kindness and strength are not opposites; they are one and the same. This love, in its simplest form, has taught me to value the everyday moments of connection. It is about being present, appreciating life as it unfolds, and always choosing to show up with love and care, whether in the quiet moments or the most challenging ones. And that is a lesson I try to live every day, not just with my family, but with everyone I meet. Kindness can surprise us in the most unexpected places – especially when it brings us back to where our story began.

BEYOND THE ICE

Becoming a mother - Love from the very beginning

The purest form of love I have ever known began quietly, before either of my children were born. From the moment I was pregnant with my children, I felt an overwhelming sense of connection. I talked to them, played music, and nourished my body as a way of caring for theirs. It was not about perfection; it was about intention. I was already loving them through attention, care, and presence.

When I gave birth, that love deepened instantly. I looked into their faces and knew, without question, that I would spend my life trying to protect, guide, and encourage them. Not just in the early days, but always.

What I have learned is that love doesn't stop as they grow older. It simply changes form. It is in the reminders to rest when they are tired, the boundaries I set to keep them grounded, and the quiet checking in to make sure they are okay. It is in knowing when to step in and when to simply be nearby.

Motherhood taught me that love is not loud. It lives in the ongoing, ordinary choices that hold someone through every stage of life. That same kind of love is what I try to bring into all of my relationships. Steady. Present. Rooted in care.

A return to India - Rediscovering love and connection

Kindness has shaped my life in unexpected ways, from the warmth of my Italian family to the lessons learned in extreme conditions. But one of the most profound experiences of kindness came when I returned to the place where my story began.

In 2019, I returned briefly to the place where my story began - a convent in India, where I had spent the first two years of my life. What I encountered there was not memory, but something far more powerful - pure, unconditional kindness. The nuns welcomed me without hesitation, as though no time had passed. We did not all speak the same language, but kindness doesn't need translation. Their embrace reminded me that love doesn't require explanation; sometimes, it simply meets you where you are.

That encounter left something quiet but powerful inside me. It reminded me that even when we feel disconnected from our origins, love can still find its way back to us. I did not yet realise how deeply that visit would shape my understanding of belonging and identity. But in time, it became a thread that led me closer to a deeper sense of truth and wholeness.

Kindness as a legacy

Every act of kindness, no matter how small, leaves an imprint. Whether it is someone braving the cold to help, a leader making space for another voice, or a nun opening her arms to a child she once held – these moments matter. They build connection, even in silence.

It doesn't require grand gestures or perfect timing. Kindness lives in the every day; in how we show up, how we listen, how we reach out when someone stumbles. It is not passive. It is a choice we make, again and again.

And when we do, we leave something behind. A legacy, not of achievements or titles, but of how we made others feel. Whether in an Arctic storm, a corporate meeting, or the quiet halls of an Indian convent, kindness moves past boundaries. It reminds people they are seen, valued, and worthy of love.

Kindness doesn't have to be dramatic. It just has to be real. A hand on a shoulder. A question that says, *"Are you okay?"* A willingness to sit with someone in silence. These moments do not just help others – they shape *us*. They become the legacy we leave behind.

Reflection Prompt

Think back to a time when a small act of kindness shifted something in you.

Did it change how you felt, how you saw the situation, or how connected you felt to others?

What would it look like to offer that same kindness to someone else this week?

Call to Action

Choose one small act of kindness you can offer today.

It could be a moment of patience, a message of encouragement, or simply asking someone how they are, and really listening.

Kindness begins in the everyday. Let it start with you.

Final Thought

Kindness does not need to be loud to be life changing.

It lives in presence, in patience, and in the quiet choice to care when no one is watching.

What stays with others is not what we achieve, but how we made them feel.

Even the smallest gesture can ripple outward, shaping lives in ways we may never fully see.

Notes

BEYOND THE ICE

CHAPTER 1

Resilience - Thriving through adversity

"Do not judge me by my success, judge me by how many times I fell down and got back up again" - **Nelson Mandela**

Redefining strength

In this chapter, we explore what resilience really means. It is not about being flawless, fearless, or endlessly strong. True resilience is found in the quiet decision to keep going, even when things are uncertain or difficult. it is not about having all the answers, but about the willingness to rise again, especially when it would be easier to give up.

Resilience in the Arctic

People often associate resilience with relentless forward motion, with pushing through no matter the cost. The Arctic taught me something different. It showed up in unexpected moments, when the harsh winds and freezing temperatures made every step a battle, but the hardest part was not always the cold. Sometimes, the most courageous thing we could do was to stop, rest, reassess, and allow ourselves the space to recover. Those pauses weren't setbacks; they were necessary. That is when I realised resilience means knowing when to gather your strength so you can rise again with intention.

Resilience beyond the ice

What I learned in the Arctic did not stay there, it followed me back into everyday life.

In the workplace, too, resilience means adapting, rebuilding, and continuing forward, even when the path is unclear. In my career, I have faced organisational upheaval, felt uncertainty as I took a leap into entrepreneurship, and picked myself up after setbacks. It is in those uncertain moments that resilience thrives, especially when we allow ourselves to lean on others instead of doing it all alone.

Resilience - A quiet strength

What I have discovered is that resilience is not the absence of hardship. It is the quiet force that helps us endure life's storms and rise stronger. Often, it is not loud or dramatic. It is the soft whisper that says, "*Try again,*" even when you feel like giving up.

This kind of strength is forged in difficult moments, when the world feels unkind, when the way forward is uncertain. It is built through small, deliberate choices: standing up after a fall, taking one more step when everything feels heavy, and holding onto self-belief when doubt surrounds you.

True resilience is not about pushing through blindly. It is about rising with awareness, finding light in the darkest corners, and discovering that thriving is possible, even when the odds feel stacked against you.

The essence of resilience

At its heart, resilience is about adapting and rising through adversity. It is the willingness to learn from setbacks, the courage to stay true to yourself when it would be easier to shrink, and the strength to embrace vulnerability without losing your core.

It doesn't always look impressive from the outside. Sometimes, it is simply the quiet decision to keep showing up, even when everything inside you is telling you to stop. Sometimes, the bravest thing you can do is stay in motion, believe in your worth, and take up space in a world that may not offer it freely.

A personal journey of resilience

When I look back on my life, resilience was not a choice, it was a necessity. It was there in moments of rejection, when I had to hold onto my worth despite feeling invisible. It surfaced in places where I did not belong, pushing me to carve out space when none was offered. And it was tested in moments of deep uncertainty, when even one step forward felt like defiance.

Resilience is not born in comfort; it is shaped by challenge. Every obstacle left its imprint, not only on what I could do, but on who I was becoming. Sometimes, it meant raising my voice above doubt. Other times, it meant finding calm in silence when the world was too loud.

What I have come to understand is this: resilience is personal, but its power is universal. it is not about having a plan. It is about choosing to keep going when you don't. Our struggles may shape us, but they do not get to define us.

BEYOND THE ICE

The Arctic - A test of body, mind and team

When I first heard about the opportunity to join an all-female team for a 100-kilometre trek across Baffin Island in the Arctic Circle, I knew I had to seize it. Among more than 100 employees who applied, I was selected to be part of something extraordinary. The mission was to challenge perceptions around diversity and inclusion, but for me, it was also something deeply personal. As well as defying the status quo, it was about testing my limits, finding my strength, and discovering who I was beneath all the labels.

As women, we are often defined by the roles we carry: wife, mother, entrepreneur, carer – but who are we beyond them? How do we evolve without losing ourselves? That is what the Arctic offered me; a chance to strip everything back. To step away from the noise and ask, *"Who am I, really?"*

In that frozen, relentless landscape, survival was the goal, but self-discovery became the reward. The cold, the silence, the physical challenge, it all forced me to confront myself. My strengths. My fears. My limits. And in doing so, I found a depth of resilience I hadn't known was there.

The Training - Beyond the comfort zone

Preparing for the Arctic was like stepping into uncharted territory. It meant pushing myself physically and mentally in ways I had never experienced before. I considered myself fit, but this was a new level. Training sessions involved dragging tyres up and down hills, simulating the sled-pulling we would face on the ice. On rainy mornings, when every muscle screamed for rest, I learned that perseverance starts long before you reach the Arctic.

And now, as I train for Everest Base Camp, I am reminded of that same truth. Resilience doesn't begin at the summit; it begins in the small, disciplined choices made long before the challenge starts.

We also spent hours in industrial freezers to acclimatise to sub-zero temperatures, standing still in the cold, learning how our bodies and minds would react. But more than physical training, we were building something else - trust.

We did not compete. We connected. We lifted each other, checked in on each other, and built relationships that quickly became lifelines. That is when I realised, resilience is not always about individual strength. It is about the strength we find when we stand side by side.

Into the Arctic

The Arctic greeted us with blistering winds, freezing temperatures, and a savage landscape that seemed designed to test us. The reality was far harsher than anything we could have trained for. Dealing with the cold and the wind chill was not just challenging, it was disorienting, exhausting, and at times overwhelming.

Yet, amid the chaos, something powerful emerged - our collective resilience.

We quickly learned to rely on one another. Eden stepped forward with clear decision-making. Cathy became our go-to for tent construction. Carole focused on navigation and strategy. Sophie lightened even the heaviest moments with her sense of humour. My own role became one of creating warmth; both by tending to the fire and by offering quiet encouragement when energy dipped or doubt crept in.

Leadership, like resilience, often means being a steady source of comfort and energy for others. In those freezing conditions, I discovered that resilience was not just about pushing through physically. It was about recognising when someone else needed a boost and stepping in without hesitation.

Overcoming the Arctic was not about heroic solo effort. It was about the strengths we brought together. It was about learning to trust one another in a setting where trust could mean survival.

Vulnerability under Arctic skies

In the Arctic, every layer, both physical and emotional, felt heavy. But as the days passed, we began to find strength not just in endurance, but in openness. Moments of quiet companionship, a knowing glance, or someone silently sharing a few extra snacks when you'd clearly hit a wall, these were the gestures that held us together.

As we grew more connected, so did our willingness to speak the things we often kept buried. One teammate opened up about feeling like an imposter. Another quietly admitted that a past failure still haunted her. These were not dramatic confessions, just quiet truths spoken into the cold.

What moved me was not just the courage it took to share. It was how we responded, with presence. No one rushed to fix or explain. We simply listened, offering space for honesty without judgement. In that space, our vulnerabilities became bridges, not barriers.

By the time the stars stretched endlessly above us and the snow reflected their silent light, something had shifted. We were no longer a group of individuals navigating an extreme environment. We had become a team, bound not just by our shared goal, but by the trust we built in the most human of ways.

Unpredictable challenges

We thought we were ready. We had trained hard, prepared meticulously, and braced ourselves for what the Arctic might bring. But the landscape had its own plans. Winds surged to 80 kilometres per hour, wiping out our visibility in minutes. Polar bears remained a distant but very real threat. The cold was not just sharp, it was consuming. It reached deep into your bones, challenging not just your body but your spirit.

Frostbite became a constant worry, and hidden crevasses turned each step into a calculated risk. We were reminded, again and again, that no matter how strong the plan, the environment would always test it.

In many ways, it felt like leading a project at work. You begin with clarity and optimism, a plan drawn with care, only to watch timelines stretch, key resources vanish, and unexpected roadblocks appear. The terrain shifts, just as it does in the boardroom or in life, demanding new footing with every step.

But true resilience doesn't come from perfect preparation. It comes from how you adapt when certainty disappears. Sometimes the storm is outside you, in the weather or the workplace. And sometimes, it rises from within: doubts, fears, the voice that whispers, "You're not strong enough."

The Arctic taught me that both storms matter. The external and the internal. And resilience is not built by avoiding either. It grows when you meet both with presence, flexibility, and a willingness to keep moving forward, even when the path ahead is unclear.

Carrying each other - When resilience means leaning in

One of the hardest moments came when Rose began showing signs of Arctic shock. Her body could no longer generate enough heat to stay safe. Her energy was gone, and her coordination started to slip. Stopping was not an option. Turning back was not possible either.

So, we carried her. We shared her pulk weight, took over her camp duties, made sure she ate, and wrapped her in every spare layer we had. Her tent buddy Gaby did not sleep that night, staying close, gently covering her nose with a gloved hand when it started turning waxy white from the cold.

In that moment, resilience was not about personal strength or endurance. It was about presence and collective responsibility: staying attuned to someone else's struggle and acting before words were even needed. What happened in that tent stayed with us long after. We weren't there to witness it in the moment, but we heard about it later, when Rose finally began to recover and Gaby shared what she had done to keep her safe through the night. It changed how we saw resilience.

It reminded us that true strength doesn't always show up in big, visible ways. Sometimes it is in a quiet act of vigilance, a willingness to stay awake through the night for someone else's safety, or the instinct to reach out when someone can't ask for help.

We realised that true strength is not always about moving forward alone. it is about recognising when someone is falling behind and choosing to slow down, carry extra, or simply be there in the silence. That is what held us together when the cold was biting and the days felt endless.

As we trekked across glaciers near Mount Asgard, the edge of the Arctic Circle, once a distant point on the map, came into view. After ten days and nights on the ice, we crossed the finish line, a group of ordinary women achieving the extraordinary.

But the greatest reward was not the destination, it was the transformation along the way. The Arctic had stripped us back to our core, revealing not just our endurance but our willingness to carry one another through. Strength was not about being the toughest. It was about trust – about choosing to take the next step, especially when everything in you wanted to stop.

And that is what resilience truly is. Not a moment of victory, but a journey of choosing to rise, again and again.

BEYOND THE ICE

Finding strength in small wins

The Arctic was the ultimate test of resilience. The cold sank to sub-zero temperatures, and the wind clawed at every ounce of warmth and resolve. Each day was a battle, not just against the elements or physical exhaustion, but against our own doubts.

The cutting cold seeped through every layer of gear, turning even the simplest movements into monumental tasks. The sleds, packed with supplies, felt heavier with each step, as though they carried the weight of our fears and frustrations. Blizzard conditions erased the horizon, and the vast emptiness played tricks on our minds. Every step forward was a quiet act of defiance against the voice that whispered, *"You won't make it."*

It was not always the dramatic moments that tested us. Often, it was the slow, creeping wear of exhaustion. One evening, after hours of pushing through the wind, we finally stopped to set up camp. I paused for just a second, gripping the handle of my sled, willing my body to move. *Just a moment to catch my breath,* I told myself.

But in the Arctic, hesitation is dangerous. The cold doesn't wait. If you stop for too long, it claims you.

Around me, the others were already moving with instinctive rhythm, staking poles into the ice, melting snow for water, adjusting their layers. The longer I stood there, the harder it became to start again.

This is where resilience is tested, not always at breaking points, but in those quiet moments when stopping feels easier than continuing.

I forced myself to move. One foot in front of the other. Unrolling the tent. Securing the ropes. Stretching stiff fingers to fumble with clips that refused to budge. It was not heroic. It was not dramatic. But it mattered. It was a decision, a small, deliberate choice to keep going when everything in me wanted to stop.

That night, as I crawled into my sleeping bag, exhausted but proud, I realised something: mental resilience is built in these invisible moments. The ones no one else sees.

Celebrating small wins

In those extreme conditions, resilience was not about monumental breakthroughs. It was about finding strength in the tiniest victories. When the wind stilled for just a few moments, it felt like a gift. A warm drink after hours of trekking became a rare luxury. Helping each other anchor tent poles into frozen ground was not just practical, it became a quiet act of unity.

Evenings around the fire were more than a chance to rest. The flicker of the flames against the ice became a backdrop for something deeper: connection. As we shared stories and laughter, we recharged in a way no meal or break ever could.

What stayed with me most was how those campfire bonds carried us beyond the firelight. When the wind roared again or the sleds grew heavier, we weren't alone. We were a team, tethered by something stronger than rope, shared experience and trust.

Those late-night conversations laid the foundation for something lasting. One story at a time, one small gesture at a time, we became stronger. And when one of us started to falter, the rest did not wait to be asked. We stepped in, instinctively, because resilience grows stronger when it is shared.

Lessons from the ice

The Arctic taught me that resilience is not about avoiding hardship. it is about meeting it head-on and finding meaning within it. Sometimes, it is not about making bold moves, but simply taking the next step, even when everything in you wants to stop. Strength doesn't always arrive as a roar.

Sometimes, it is the steady voice inside that reminds you, *"Keep going. You've come this far."*

I learned that resilience is not a solo pursuit. It grows through connection, in the hands that support us, the voices that ground us, and the shared moments that remind us we're not alone. The Arctic stripped away all pretence. It left only our truest selves. And in that raw space, we found a deeper strength, not just individually, but together.

Resilience looks different for everyone. What stretches one person may barely register for another, but each experience is valid. The Arctic showed me that resilience is not about surviving the storm, it is about allowing it to shape us. It is about recognising every small step as a win, and seeing that even in the bleakest moments, connection and care can light the way forward.

Workplace - Building resilience in organisations

In the workplace, resilience is not just an individual trait. It is a culture. High-performing organisations aren't defined by their ability to avoid disruption, but by how they respond, adapt, and recover from it. Resilient teams manage risk effectively and stay grounded through uncertainty.

Resilience at work is not passive; it is an active, ongoing process. At its core are three elements: **anticipation**, **response**, and **adaptation**.

Resilient organisations anticipate change. They stay attuned to shifts in their environment, industry, and workforce. This foresight helps them adapt before a crisis hits. Diverse teams play a critical role here; drawing on different perspectives allows for earlier identification of emerging challenges and more nuanced planning.

When disruption does strike, resilient teams know how to respond. They do not panic or retreat. They act, drawing on a mix of expertise and creativity. Diversity matters here too. When a challenge is viewed from many angles, solutions are broader, bolder, and more effective.

But perhaps the most powerful aspect of organisational resilience is adaptation. True resilience is not about bouncing back to where you were. It is about learning, growing, and evolving. The best teams reflect on what happened, carry the lessons forward, and emerge stronger.

This cycle - *anticipate, respond, adapt* - builds not only resilience, but momentum. It helps organisations move with intention, even in uncertainty. When diversity is embedded in this process, teams are more agile, inclusive, and prepared for the unknown.

The role of diversity in organisational resilience

Diversity plays a vital role in building resilience, especially in times of uncertainty. it is not just about representation or ticking boxes. It is about creating a culture where different voices are heard, valued, and actively included in decision-making.

When organisations embrace diversity, they unlock broader capabilities in three essential areas of resilience: **anticipation**, **response**, and **adaptation**.

First, diverse teams are better at anticipating change. People with different backgrounds bring varied perspectives, which helps identify emerging risks and spot shifts that might otherwise be missed. Whether it is a new market trend or a potential disruption, a team with diverse experiences is often more attuned and responsive.

Second, coping with challenges becomes more effective when diverse ideas and experiences are at the table. In moments of pressure, teams that include multiple perspectives are more likely to come up with creative and well-rounded solutions. They ask different questions, challenge assumptions, and collaborate in ways that strengthen outcomes.

Finally, adaptation. The ability to evolve after a crisis, to learn from what happened and apply those lessons going forward, is critical. A diverse team contributes to this process by reflecting from different vantage points, helping the organisation not just recover, but grow. They bring insights that lead to better systems, stronger cultures, and more inclusive ways of working.

Resilience thrives in environments where differences are respected and used to fuel progress. It is not enough to hire for diversity; we must lead in a way that ensures every voice is welcomed, listened to, and able to shape the future.

These core principles apply beyond business. Whether within a family, community, or expedition team, resilience is strengthened when we embrace diverse strengths, share responsibility, and move forward together.

Leadership in action

I recall one particular workshop where a senior leader opened up about the difficulties of driving a diversity initiative within their organisation. What struck me was how familiar their story felt. It reminded me of a time when I joined a new team and quickly noticed a pattern I'd seen before.

In that team, it was the long-serving members whose voices held the most weight. They were trusted, familiar, and often the first to be heard in meetings. For someone new, even after several months, it could feel like your input was an afterthought – not because your ideas lacked merit, but because tenure had quietly become the default marker of value.

BEYOND THE ICE

During the workshop, I shared my own experience. I spoke about how I built trust over time, not by pushing louder, but by contributing consistently. I offered the leader some practical suggestions: try rotating meeting facilitators, invite newer voices to speak first, or create quiet moments where everyone can write and share ideas without interruption.

What stayed with me was how willing they were to listen. A few weeks later, they got in touch to say those small changes had already made a difference. Not only had the initiative gained traction, but the team dynamic had started to shift. Trust had grown and so had engagement.

That conversation reminded me that leadership is not about always having the answers. It is about making space for others. It is about paying attention to who is not speaking, who's being overlooked, and how to shift the balance so that everyone has the chance to contribute.

Lesson: In leadership, resilience is not reactive. It is a culture built through daily intention and awareness.

When we commit to adaptability, empathy, and continuous learning, we do not just survive disruption, we grow because of it.

Personal Story - Rebuilding from scratch: my UK journey

When I first moved to the UK, I had nothing but a piece of luggage and a deep determination to start a new life. Everything was unfamiliar: the language, the customs, the pace of it all. I had no safety net, no connections, and no certainty. But I did not come to question the decision. I came to make it work.

My first role was as an au pair, caring for children while attending university part-time. I later became a nanny, balancing study and work as I began to build a life from the ground up. There were no shortcuts. Every new word I learned, every essay I submitted, every late night of revision after putting the children to bed, they all became part of the foundation I was laying.

Eventually, I stepped into the corporate world. Each opportunity came through persistence, not luck, and through the belief that my effort would eventually be seen. I knew there was no way back, only a way forward. I was ready to do whatever it took to create the future I had envisioned.

That journey taught me that resilience is not always loud or visible. It lives in quiet acts of discipline, in showing up even when things are hard, and in trusting that each step, no matter how small, is building something meaningful. I did not just start over. I rebuilt, with courage, clarity, and an unshakable belief that I was meant to thrive

BEYOND THE ICE

Entrepreneurship and the power of the pivot

Two years after the expedition, with courage and determination, I took another leap. I left the corporate world to start my own business as a keynote speaker and facilitator. At first, everything aligned. The momentum was exhilarating. I was delivering in-person speeches, connecting with diverse audiences, and enjoying a healthy turnover.

Then, COVID-19 hit.

The world shut down, and with it, so did my business. My calendar of events disappeared overnight. While others continued working from home, I faced the harsh reality of an empty schedule and uncertain income.

But I did not panic. I adapted.

I leaned into discomfort and chose to pivot. I transitioned my content online, began delivering webinars, and reconnected with former clients to offer something new. It was not easy, but slowly, things began to shift.

What started as a way to stay afloat became a launchpad for growth. I created new workshops, deepened my focus on Diversity and Inclusion, and reached clients across the globe. This period did not just test my business, it transformed it. I learned to trust my creativity, to stay present in uncertainty, and to hold onto my purpose even when the path forward was unclear.

BEYOND THE ICE

That is what resilience looks like in business. Not certainty, but conviction. Not knowing all the steps but committing to take the next one.

BEYOND THE ICE

Key lessons from the journey What the Arctic, the workplace, and my personal life have taught me is that resilience is not about facing hardship alone, it is how we *rise, rebuild, and keep going* when life challenges us

I have learned that true resilience is rooted in connection. Around the Arctic campfire, when our bodies were cold but our hearts full from shared stories, I realised that trust and support can carry us further than strength alone. When we open up and let others in, we build bonds that make us stronger, not just as individuals, but as a team.

I have also learned that resilience is built one step at a time. It is not always bold or visible. Often, it is in the quiet victories, a shared laugh after a gruelling trek, a moment of stillness in the wind, or a sip of hot tea that reminds us we're still human. Those small wins became fuel when motivation felt far away.

In business, adaptability became a lifeline. The pandemic did not just test my business; it reshaped it. Pivoting to virtual delivery was not a backup plan, it became a new path forward. It taught me that growth often begins where certainty ends.

And above all, reflection has changed how I see setbacks. They no longer feel like barriers, they feel like invitations. Invitations to pause, to ask, "What is this teaching me?" That mindset shift, from fear to curiosity, has been one of the most powerful lessons of all.

Reflection Prompt

Think back to a time when you overcame something difficult.

What helped you rise in that moment?

What did that experience teach you about your own resilience?

Call to Action

Cultivating resilience in everyday life

Resilience is not built in the big moments alone. It grows in small choices, made each day.
Today, take a moment to notice one quiet way you kept going, even when it was hard.
Then, think of someone who may need that same encouragement. A message, a call, or simply being present can make all the difference.
Resilience becomes stronger when we carry it together.

Final Thought

Resilience has shaped every part of my journey. From arriving in the UK with little more than hope, to standing on frozen ground in the Arctic, to rebuilding a business during a global shutdown.
It has never looked like certainty or confidence from the outside. Most often, it has looked like quiet determination, shaky first steps, and the belief that I could begin again.

BEYOND THE ICE

That is what resilience truly is. Not perfection, but persistence. Not having it all figured out, but choosing to rise, even when you do not know how.

And in that quiet choice, made again and again, we do not just survive. We grow.

BEYOND THE ICE

Notes

CHAPTER 6

Courage - Facing fear with action

"I am no longer accepting the things I cannot change. I am changing the things I cannot accept."-
Angela Davis

The heart of courage

Courage doesn't only live in dramatic, heroic moments. It reveals itself in the quiet, everyday choices to take a stand, embrace change, or push past fear. Courage is not the absence of fear, but the decision to act anyway. Often, it lives where vulnerability meets determination and where action turns fear into strength.

For me, courage has taken many forms. It looked like standing on the edge of a frozen river in the Arctic, stepping forward while my heart raced with uncertainty. It showed up in the workplace when I supported a leader who dared to challenge the status quo despite resistance. And perhaps most personally, it was the quiet bravery of moving to England alone, determined to rebuild a life that felt like my own.

In this chapter, we will walk through each of these spaces, the Arctic, the workplace, and the deeply personal terrain of starting over, and discover how courage is often born in discomfort, nurtured in connection, and lived one small, bold step at a time.

Sometimes, courage is about speaking up. Other times, it is about stepping into unfamiliar territory, like I did in the Arctic, where fear was not an abstract concept but something I had to face head-on.

BEYOND THE ICE

The Arctic - Courage in vulnerability

The Arctic strips away pretences, leaving only raw reality and presence.

On a still, luminous day in Baffin Island's Akshayuk Pass, we stood at the edge of the Weasel River, its frozen surface glinting under the soft light of an Arctic sun. The cliffs around us stood like ancient sentinels, their jagged peaks dusted with snow. For a moment, the landscape seemed timeless, almost serene. But beauty here can be deceptive. Beneath the fragile ice, currents ran fast and deep, and hidden crevasses turned each step into a gamble, some deep enough to swallow us whole.

As we prepared to cross, crampons crunching into the surface, every movement demanded focus. There was no room for error. My heart raced as I stood frozen at the edge, doubt swirling. What if the ice gave way? What if I slipped?

Then Mandy reached out her hand and simply said, *"I have got you."* That small gesture changed everything. I was not alone. We stepped forward together, crampons biting into the fragile surface, the silence broken only by the creak of ice and our steady breath.

Courage emerged not in the absence of fear, but *through* it. In that one act of reaching forward, of trusting one another, of moving anyway, I understood that courage is rarely a solo act. It is born in connection, in the quiet moments when someone believes in you just enough to help you believe in yourself.

BEYOND THE ICE

Building bonds in the Arctic

As we ventured deeper into the Arctic, I realised that courage was not just faced alone, it was forged together.

At first, we were a group of strangers hiding behind both literal and emotional masks. Every inch of our bodies was covered, faces obscured by layers of clothing and goggles. Our conversations were reduced to muffled voices and the occasional nod. Beneath all that insulation, each of us was carrying quiet fears: *Am I strong enough? Do I belong here?*

We gathered in the tent, not because a single danger threatened us, but because after six days of walking with little sleep and mounting exhaustion, we were close to our limit. If even one of us had gone down, we knew the rest might not have had the strength to carry on. It was not just about staying in the fight, it was about holding each other up when we were all stretched thin.

Stories began to surface, quiet, personal truths we hadn't expected to share. Someone spoke of always needing to prove their worth. Another recalled the weight of being underestimated for most of their life. We did not rush to respond or offer advice. What unfolded was not just a conversation. It was recognition. We saw each other beyond the layers, beyond roles or expectations. In that honesty, we found a new kind of strength.

By morning, we were no longer a collection of individuals but a united team, bound by the courage to be seen and heard. The raw honesty of that night stayed with us, carrying us through the icy valleys, the biting cold, and the endless expanse of snow and ice.

Courage creates ripples

Sometimes, courage is not just about the individual. It is about how one brave act can spark another. I'll never forget my first paid speaking event. I had crafted a story I cared deeply about, and as I looked out at the audience, I saw eyes light up, nods of recognition, and a sense that my words were landing. My message had been received.

At the end of the session, a woman approached me. "Your story," she said, "is one of courage and resilience. It gave me the push I needed." Weeks later, I received a message from her. "I saw you speak at that event, and it inspired me so much. I took my car and drove on the motorway for the first time in years. I'd had an accident before and was never able to go back, but your story gave me the courage to try again."

That message reminded me that courage rarely begins with grand gestures. Often, it starts with one small, impossibly brave step. The courage to get behind the wheel. The courage to speak your truth. The courage to share something real in the hope it might help someone else.

In fact, this book is a result of that same process. It has been shaped by the decision to share my own story, a commitment that began ten years ago, when I first returned from the Arctic. Not just to find healing for myself, but to offer a path forward for others too.

BEYOND THE ICE

Workplace - Taking a stand for diversity

Courage in the workplace is not always about bold declarations or sweeping changes. Often, it is about making a quiet but powerful decision to stand for what's right, even when it is uncomfortable or unpopular.

Just as we leaned on each other in the Arctic to find courage, leadership often requires that same willingness to take a step forward, even in the face of resistance.

During a diversity and inclusion initiative, I worked closely with a senior leader who faced significant pushback from their team. The resistance was not loud or overt. It showed up in disengaged body language, side comments like "Do we really need this?" and reluctance to adopt new policies designed to create a more inclusive culture.

I remember one meeting in particular. The leader presented a proposal to launch mentorship programmes for underrepresented groups. The room fell quiet. A few people avoided eye contact, and some questioned whether such initiatives were necessary, describing them as "divisive" or "unfair."

It would have been easy for the leader to retreat, to water down the proposal in order to keep the peace. But they didn't. Instead, they stood their ground and calmly addressed the concerns. They explained why the initiative was not about giving special treatment but about creating equity and levelling the playing field. They shared data about the barriers faced by underrepresented employees and, more powerfully, shared a personal story about why inclusion mattered to them.

That vulnerability shifted something. While not everyone in the room changed their perspective immediately, the atmosphere softened. Dialogue opened. Gradually, more team members began asking questions, offering feedback, and engaging with the initiative. What had started as quiet resistance began to evolve into active participation.

That experience reminded me that courage at work doesn't always come in dramatic moments. Often, it shows up in the steady commitment to do what's right, even when it is hard. It is about holding your ground, sharing your 'why,' and staying the course when progress feels slow.

The moment of courage

In 2024, I was invited to deliver a keynote at a corporate leadership conference attended by about 500 professionals. During my talk, I explained the value of authenticity, particularly for leaders. I shared that if I were a CEO or a leader, I'd want to create genuine connections with my team by being open about who I am: no façade, no masks.

For example, if I identify as part of the LGBTQ+ community or have a deeply personal story, and I feel comfortable sharing it, I believe doing so can create a ripple effect of connection and openness within the team. Of course, this is not to say that everyone should feel obliged to share deeply personal aspects of their lives. It is about making space for those who choose to and understanding the power of leading by example.

BEYOND THE ICE

During that session, something extraordinary happened. A man, whom I'll call Ted, stood up. He had been a leader at his company for over 29 years, respected and admired by his peers. With a trembling voice but steady determination, he shared something deeply personal - he was part of the LGBTQ+ community. For many in the audience, it was a surprise. But more importantly, it was a moment of courage.

Ted's openness shifted the energy in the room. What had been a conversation about policies and inclusion became a conversation about people, empathy, and authenticity. His courage not only inspired others to reflect on their own stories but also created a sense of safety and belonging.

Ted's act of courage highlighted an essential truth about leadership - vulnerability is not a weakness; it is a tool for creating authentic connections. It is a gateway to trust and connection. Leaders who embrace vulnerability create ripple effects of trust and belonging, inspiring others to step into their own courage.

Later that evening, at the restaurant, I experienced the ripple effect of his courage. About 25 people approached me, eager to share their own personal truths. Ted's act of vulnerability had opened the door for others to step into their own authenticity.

Lesson: Courage in leadership is not about having all the answers; it is about being authentic, taking a stand, and showing others the strength in vulnerability. When leaders step forward with honesty, they create opportunities for others to do the same, building an environment of trust and connection.

Courage in honest conversations

Courage often hides in quieter moments. Giving honest feedback can be just as daunting as stepping onto a stage.

Courage is not just about leading teams. It is also about the small, often invisible acts of honesty and care that help others grow. During my ten years at Toastmasters International, where I earned my Distinguished Toastmaster (DTM) recognition after just four years, I learned that leadership and courage often go hand in hand. That journey was full of lessons, but one moment stands out more than any speech I ever gave.

As an evaluator, part of my role was to provide feedback that could help others grow. On one occasion, I had to address a speaker whose accent was so strong that it was difficult for the audience to understand their message. It was a delicate situation. I did not want to discourage them or make them feel unwelcome, but I also knew that honesty, when delivered with care, could be a gift.

I took a deep breath and said, "Your passion shines through in your speech, and it is clear you have an important story to share. However, there were moments when your message was a little hard to follow because of your accent. I believe with some focused practice on pronunciation or pace; you can make your incredible ideas even more impactful."

Their response surprised me. Instead of feeling disheartened, they thanked me for being honest and for giving them a practical path forward. Over time, they worked on their clarity and became one of the most engaging speakers in the group.

That exchange reminded me that courage is not always about grand gestures. Sometimes, it is about saying what needs to be said, with empathy and intention. Whether in a professional or personal setting, honest feedback delivered with care can be transformative.

Giving and receiving feedback requires vulnerability on both sides. It is a reminder that courage is not just about taking risks for yourself. It is also about helping others step into their potential. And it works both ways. The courage to offer feedback must be met with the courage to receive it openly.

Personal - Moving to England - A leap of faith

Courage is often the catalyst for transformation. When I decided to move to England alone, it was not a carefully calculated decision. It was a leap of faith. There was no clear road map, no familiar faces, just a quiet, determined belief that I needed to begin again.

More than a physical relocation, it became an emotional reckoning.

Leaving France was not just a change of address. It was a declaration of self-worth. I was saying, "I want more than this. I deserve more than this." I was leaving behind not just a country, but the labels, expectations, and limiting beliefs that had been projected onto me since childhood.

At the time, I did not call it courage. I called it necessity. But now, I realise it was one of the most courageous decisions I have ever made. I arrived in the UK with a deep desire to rebuild, not just a life, but a version of myself I could fully own.

The courage did not end when I arrived at Paddington Station. It showed up in the everyday. In learning a new language. In navigating cultural differences. In figuring out how to pay rent, enrol in university, and apply for jobs, all in a system I did not fully understand. Every small decision, from asking for help to walking into interviews that felt far beyond my reach, took more bravery than I gave myself credit for at the time.

BEYOND THE ICE

And perhaps the hardest part? Doing it all without anyone who looked like me, sounded like me, or fully understood what I had left behind.

That journey taught me that courage doesn't always look like big declarations or dramatic leaps. Sometimes, it is simply choosing to start again when everything feels unfamiliar. It is building something from nothing. It is trusting that, despite the fear, you will find your way.

The first weeks were tough. I did not know anyone, and the unfamiliarity of a new culture, language, and environment was overwhelming. I remember the smell of the city streets, the silence of the evenings, the weight of loneliness pressing down as I tried to find my footing in a world that felt both exciting and disorienting. But each small step forward – understanding a word in English, navigating a train journey, making my first friend – became a quiet act of courage. And not once did I regret the decision. I never looked back. I knew it was right from the start.

While I was not a refugee – I had a French passport, no visa restrictions, and the freedom to travel – I often carried the same emotional weight. I hadn't fled war. But I had fled a kind of erasure. A life where I couldn't fully be myself.

I once coached someone who had arrived in the UK years earlier as a refugee. They had since rebuilt their life, found work in community outreach, and were thriving in many ways. But during one of our conversations, they said something I'll never forget, "People assume I came here to be safe. But really, I came to breathe."

That line moved me deeply. Because safety is not just about physical survival, it is about emotional space. Freedom. Dignity.

Their story was different from mine in every meaningful way. And yet, I recognised something. We both understood what it meant to start again. To build identity in a place that did not always know what to do with us. To let go of one version of ourselves in order to become another.

Even within my own family, I saw the contrast. My husband moved from Italy to the UK for opportunity. It was strategic, hopeful, calculated. My decision felt different. Not forced, but not fully chosen either. More like a quiet escape from the version of me I had outgrown.

What no one tells you about courage is that it does not always come with a label. It does not always announce itself. Sometimes, it is not about fleeing or chasing. It is about choosing not to stay, even when you do not yet know where you are going.

Turning fear into action

Courage is not about eliminating fear. It is about moving forward through it. When I arrived in the UK, I signed up for language classes, worked odd jobs, and took every opportunity I could find. Each step (no matter how small) was part of building a foundation. That persistence, more than any single moment, was what carried me forward.

Looking back, I see that leap not as one bold moment, but as the start of many small acts of persistence.

BEYOND THE ICE

Lesson: Courage does not always roar. Sometimes it is quiet, trembling, and deeply personal. It can look like accepting help, sharing a truth, starting over, or offering honest feedback with care.

In the Arctic, it was trusting my team. In the workplace, it was standing up for what mattered. In my personal life, it was leaving behind what no longer fit and rebuilding from the ground up. Courage lives in the small, repeated choices to keep going. And when we act with courage, we do more than move forward. We invite others to do the same.

Reflection Prompt

Think of a time when you took a courageous step, even if it felt small.

What did that experience teach you about your strength?

How might you carry that lesson with you today?

Call to Action

Take one bold step…Think of a moment in your life when you acted with courage big or small. What did it reveal about your strength?

Now choose one small step today that moves you in the direction of that same courage.

It could be a conversation you've been avoiding, a story you're ready to share, or a choice that feels uncomfortable but necessary.

You do not need to feel fearless. You only need to begin.

Final Thought

Courage has shaped every part of my journey. From crossing icy rivers in the Arctic, to moving to a new country alone, to standing on a stage and sharing my story. It has rarely looked fearless. More often, it has looked like a deep breath, a trembling voice, or the quiet decision to keep going.

I have learned that courage grows through action. It gains strength each time we move forward, even with fear beside us. It is not reserved for the extraordinary. It lives in the everyday moments when we choose not to stay silent, stuck, or small.

The beauty of courage is that it multiplies. Every act of bravery creates space for others to be brave too. So whether you are stepping into the unknown or holding steady in a storm, remember this: your courage matters. Let it carry you forward. It has the power to change everything.

Notes

BEYOND THE ICE

CHAPTER 6

Trust - The fuel that powers meaningful relationships

"To be trusted is a greater compliment than to be loved."- George MacDonald

When we really tune in, we stop listening just for words and start noticing what is unspoken. The hesitation in someone's voice. The shift in posture. The silence that follows a difficult question. These subtle cues often reveal more than language alone ever could.

In this chapter, we will explore how trust is tested and shaped. It appears in the silence of the Arctic, in the pressure of leadership, and in the quiet resilience of rebuilding self-belief. Trust is not just a value. It is a daily practice.

Psychologist Albert Mehrabian's research reminds us that in emotionally charged moments, what we express through presence often matters more than what we say. In the Arctic, where our voices were often lost to the wind and cold, we had to rely on hand signals, body language, and eye contact. These gestures were more than practical. They became our language of trust.

BEYOND THE ICE

The power of non-verbal communication

One of the most underrated elements of trust is how much we communicate without speaking. In emotionally charged or uncertain situations, such as giving feedback, resolving conflict, or offering support, our tone of voice, facial expressions, and body language often reveal more than our words.

Psychologist Albert Mehrabian's research from the 1960s is often cited in communication discussions but is frequently misunderstood. His work focused specifically on how people express feelings and attitudes, not general communication.

What he found was that when someone conveys emotion and their words and tone do not align, listeners rely more heavily on non-verbal cues to interpret meaning. Facial expressions and body language play a significant role, alongside tone, pitch, and rhythm. The actual words still matter, but in emotionally charged situations, *how* something is said can carry more weight than *what* is said.

It would be inaccurate to claim that most of our communication is non-verbal, but the research does remind us of something important: when building trust and connection, presence often speaks louder than words.

These insights became deeply personal in the Arctic. With our faces covered and our voices swallowed by the wind, we had to rely on hand signals, body language, and quiet intuition. A nod, a glance, a reassuring hand, these became our main language of trust.

Over time, I came to think of this as a kind of internal compass. Whether in a meeting, with a loved one, or during a difficult conversation, we build trust not by saying more, but by showing up with intention.

Trust often reveals itself in high-stakes environments, where every decision carries weight and every action matters. It forms quietly, not through grand gestures, but through consistency, honesty, and presence. Whether standing on the edge of a frozen landscape, leading a team through complexity, or learning to trust yourself after a setback, trust becomes the quiet force that makes progress possible.

The essence of trust

Clarity lays the foundation for progress, but it is trust that sustains momentum when things get difficult. In the Arctic, clarity of purpose got us to the starting line. But it was trust that carried us through storms, biting cold, and moments of doubt.

Trust is not a luxury. It is the heartbeat of connection, the invisible thread that holds people together when certainty disappears. It is not built through grand gestures, but through small, daily moments of consistency, courage, and vulnerability.

In this chapter, we will explore how trust evolves in extreme environments, in leadership, and within ourselves.

BEYOND THE ICE

Arctic - Trust in action

After battling the temptation to stay cocooned in my sleeping bag that morning, I moved cautiously. In the Arctic's subzero temperatures, even the smallest movement could dislodge the fine ice crystals lining the tent and create an unwelcome snowfall for my tent buddies. Getting dressed was another ordeal. My frozen clothes felt like slabs of ice against my skin and took at least twenty minutes to warm. Since Sally had left due to her ankle injury, I was now sharing the tent with two others. There was at least one silver lining: the added body heat made the nights a little more bearable.

That morning, I glanced at Grace and noticed a white patch forming on her forehead. It was a telltale sign of frostbite. With no mirrors in the Arctic, we relied on each other to spot potential dangers. Mandy and I hesitated for a moment. What if we were wrong? Should we say something? But hesitation was not an option in that environment. In those conditions, silence could be costly.

"Warm that up immediately," Mandy said, urgency clear in her voice. Grace nodded and acted quickly, trusting our observation without question. Later, she thanked us, admitting, "I didn't even realise."

That moment reinforced something I had already begun to understand. Trust is not just about speaking up. It is also about having the humility to listen. This was not only about saving Grace from the cold. It was about knowing we could rely on one another when it mattered most.

Trust in silent gestures

Trust is often built in the smallest and quietest moments.

After a strenuous day of pulling sledges across an endless expanse of snow, our visibility was reduced to the size of a small coin because of frosted goggles and fierce winds. When we finally reached base camp, exhausted, I glanced back and saw Mandy struggling in the distance.

In addition to being part of the team, Mandy was also our photographer. Her role required more than just endurance. It demanded constant sacrifice. She often stopped to capture the Arctic's raw beauty, which meant falling behind the group, facing repeated tumbles, and enduring frostnip on her fingers.

Watching her battle the elements, I was drawn to her side. Without hesitation, I grabbed the rope and shared the weight. It was not about being asked for help. It was about recognising when it was needed and stepping in.

Trust in the Arctic was not forged through heroic actions. It was shaped by small, consistent acts of solidarity. It was not just about surviving. It was what connected us and transformed a group of individuals into a unified team.

BEYOND THE ICE

Trust across cultures - Arctic reflections

In the Arctic, not all of us shared the same cultural references or ways of expressing support. Some of us relied on humour. Others stayed quiet, offering presence rather than words. We had different norms around eye contact, personal space, and how we asked for help. But very quickly, we began to read each other in new ways.

A glance. A nod. The way someone stood a little closer in the fog. These were not just gestures, they were signals of care. Even without speaking the same language in the same way, we found ways to connect. We learned to trust not because of what was said, but because of what was shown.

It reminded me that in the harshest environments, trust does not rely on words. It depends on presence. On noticing. On offering support before it is requested. And on accepting that connection does not always sound like us. Sometimes, it simply feels like being seen.

Workplace - Trust in leadership

In the workplace, trust is the foundation for collaboration, innovation, and success. But trust is not automatic, it has to be earned and nurtured, especially in leadership roles.

For a few years, I worked with a leader who often assumed they knew best. During a critical project, they bypassed the team and contacted the wrong country managers directly, issuing confusing instructions in an attempt to demonstrate control to their superiors.

The results were devastating – chaos. Confused and frustrated, country managers bypassed the leader entirely and came straight to us for clarity. This experience reinforced a crucial lesson: trust is not built on authority or control. It is earned through reliability, consistency, and genuine care. Leadership is not about asserting power; it is about inspiring confidence.

What does great leadership look like?

Some of the most impactful leaders I have encountered weren't even my direct managers. One CEO, for instance, had a profound impact on me, despite not being someone I reported to. He had a way of making everyone feel seen and valued, regardless of his position in the organisation. He created a sense of psychological safety by listening with attention, communicating openly, and encouraging accountability without blame. He once gave me a 360-degree view of my career path, helping me to see opportunities I hadn't considered before. What struck me most was the genuine care he showed, expecting nothing in return.

That kind of leadership is not something you tend to forget easily, not because it is flashy or rewarded, but because it is real.

It made me reflect on how true leadership often goes unrecognised, not driven by ego or accolades, but by a deep-seated commitment to others.

In 2024, I was invited to a ceremony celebrating Europe's most human-centric leaders. It was an evening dedicated to recognising those who go beyond their job descriptions to create inclusive, trusting environments. Seeing leadership honoured in this way was a powerful reminder that leadership is not about enforcing authority, it is about empowering others.

Bringing leadership traits into everyday practice

These are a few ways I have applied those leadership lessons in my own life.

Create psychological safety - Ask yourself, "Do my team members feel safe speaking up, sharing ideas, or admitting mistakes?" Take deliberate steps to build this safety by reacting calmly to feedback, encouraging collaboration, and showing gratitude for honesty.

When I was just starting out as a people manager, I had a small team of two. Looking back, I realise how much they actually taught me, whether they needed hand-holding or not. One of them, who had recently moved in with her partner, began arriving late and was not as bubbly as usual. I later learned through a colleague that she'd been going through a breakup but hadn't felt it was appropriate to share it with me. "*Work, not drama*," as she put it. That moment made me reflect on how open I was, and whether I had created a space where she felt she could share personal struggles without feeling judged.

Offer guidance without expecting anything in return - In my career, I have always believed that guidance should be offered freely, whether it is through the tips I share on social media, during keynotes, or in casual conversations. it is about providing support with no strings attached. There's a concept called "pay it forward," where you do something kind and instead of expecting gratitude, you simply ask the other person to do the same for someone else. it is a simple yet powerful practice that costs nothing and can make a huge difference.

In both my personal and professional life, I try to live by this principle. Offering help with no expectation of reward not only strengthens relationships, it creates a culture where generosity is passed on - a chain reaction of care. Even the smallest act can ripple outward in ways we may never see.

Make people feel seen - In meetings or one-to-one conversations, give your full attention. Recognise achievements, validate concerns, and express appreciation. A small gesture, like remembering a personal detail, can make someone feel genuinely valued. I remember speaking to a potential client who shared that his dog, Toffee, had just undergone surgery. When we spoke again a couple of months later, I asked, "How's Toffee doing?" That simple act of care turned a business exchange into a real connection. He later became a client.

Communicate openly - Transparency builds trust. Whether addressing challenges, setting expectations, or providing feedback, lead with clarity and empathy.

By applying these practices consistently, I have found that I am not just building trust in my leadership, I am creating a ripple effect that encourages others to lead with authenticity and care.

BEYOND THE ICE

Personal - Trusting yourself again

Rebuilding trust in others often begins with rebuilding trust in yourself. For years, I wrestled with self-doubt, shaped by rejection, microaggressions, and a lifetime of being told, "You will never succeed." When I started working for a new organisation, I knew I was not perfect, but I was eager to prove myself. I also recognised that I was stepping into a challenging environment. Yet, my manager seemed to doubt me from the start. I was not given the same support as others. Mistakes were magnified. I often felt dismissed before I even had the chance to show my potential.

Here is what I learned: trusting yourself does not mean pretending you have no weaknesses. It means being honest about them and still believing in your ability to grow.

I longed to join the international division, but when I shared this aspiration, I was met with skepticism. "You will never manage an international position," they said. That comment could have held me back, but instead, it became fuel for my determination. I sought out mentors, built relationships, and absorbed every bit of knowledge I could. I paid close attention to feedback, learning to separate what was useful from what was rooted in doubt or bias.

Twelve months later, I applied for the role of Account Manager in the international division. The process was rigorous, with three interviews, including one with the CEO. When I got the job, it was not just a career milestone, it was a moment of profound self-realisation. Someone had seen something in me, and I had chosen to believe in myself too.

Looking back, I see that trusting myself was not just about getting the role. It was about choosing to shape my own path, regardless of others' doubts. I also learned how to tell the difference between criticism that helps and criticism that holds you back. That trust, in myself and in those who saw my potential, became the ground I could rebuild from.

Self-trust is not about ignoring flaws or blaming others. It is about taking ownership of your growth, embracing your imperfections, and choosing to keep moving forward anyway. When we trust ourselves, we create the conditions for confidence, clarity, and momentum.

Trust begins at home

Trust is just as essential at home as it is at work. Whether we are parents, caregivers, or mentors, it is natural to want to guide the people we care about, to shield them from mistakes and clear the way forward. But I have learned that sometimes, the greatest trust we can offer is to step back and let them find their own path.

I remember a time when my daughter was preparing for an important exam. Like many parents, I encouraged her to study, sometimes with gentle reminders, other times with firmer nudges. When she did not seem fully engaged, I began to worry that she was not taking it seriously. I was tempted to intervene, to hover and monitor every move. But instead, I chose to pause. I chose to trust that when it mattered, she would take responsibility.

It was not easy. I had to resist the urge to control the outcome. But in doing so, I discovered something deeper. Trust also means believing in someone's ability to rise. In the end, she committed to the process and exceeded expectations. That experience reminded me that trust at home often means letting go. Not of care, but of control. It means offering belief, not pressure.

The lesson of trust at home

Trust is not about giving up care, it is about showing belief in someone's ability to find their own way. Whether it is a child facing exams, a partner tackling a new project, or even ourselves confronting new challenges, stepping back and trusting someone's capabilities can inspire growth and confidence far greater than constant oversight ever could.

Lesson from personal growth - That experience taught me something I would carry forward: that trusting yourself is the foundation of resilience.

Trust in crisis - When pressure tests bonds

Trust is never more visible than in a moment of crisis. It reveals the strength of relationships, the depth of leadership, and whether the bonds we have built can hold under pressure.

I learned this in the corporate world while managing a high-stakes international project. Everything had been running smoothly until, just days before a major client presentation, a serious error surfaced. It was not mine, but as the project lead, the responsibility fell on me. The atmosphere turned tense. People looked for someone to blame. I could feel it in the silence, in the glances, in the weight of unspoken questions.

In that moment, I had a choice. I could protect myself, shift blame, or stay grounded and take ownership. I chose to lead. "We will fix this," I said. "Let's focus on what we can do now." Not everyone rallied right away. One colleague walked away, needing time. That was fine. Trust does not mean instant agreement. It means space. It means patience.

Eventually, the team came back. Some returned because deadlines demanded it. Others returned because they saw I was not interested in blame, only in moving forward. We worked late into the night, rebuilt what had been broken, and delivered ahead of schedule. The client never knew what had happened behind the scenes. But the real success was not the presentation. It was the trust that held when things fell apart. Because trust in crisis is not about being perfect. It is about staying present.

Cultural nuances in trust

Trust is not universal. It is shaped by culture, context, and unspoken expectations. In some cultures, trust is built quickly through casual conversations. In others, it is earned slowly through structure and time. Misunderstanding these differences can erode trust, even when intentions are good.

Throughout my career, I have worked with teams and clients from over sixty countries. Each had its own rhythm of communication and connection. I learned that in some places, directness is appreciated as a sign of honesty. In others, it can be seen as rude or abrupt.

There is no single way to build trust, only a shared willingness to try.

Once, I was presenting a proposal during a virtual meeting with a team from a high-context culture. After I spoke, the room went quiet. I panicked. Did I offend them? Was the idea rejected? Later, a colleague explained that in their culture, silence is not avoidance. It is respect. It is reflection.

That experience reminded me of a story from *The Culture Map* by Erin Meyer. While giving a presentation in Japan, she invited questions, but no one responded. Later, she learned that in Japan, people rarely ask questions in public. Instead, they show interest through subtle gestures like eye contact or a small nod.

Whether in Tokyo, Toronto, or Tunis, trust depends on understanding the world from someone else's view. It is not about saying things perfectly. It is about showing people they matter.

Practical tips for exploring cultural nuances

Building trust across cultures begins with curiosity. I make it a point to ask questions. How do people here give feedback? How do they show respect? What does trust look like in this space?

Sometimes, building trust means adjusting how I show up. In more hierarchical cultures, involving senior leaders is not just respectful, it is essential. In other spaces, warmth and informality help to build rapport.

BEYOND THE ICE

I remember working with someone who avoided eye contact in every meeting. At first, I thought they were disengaged. But I later learned that, in their culture, avoiding direct gaze is a form of respect. That single insight changed how I approached the entire relationship.

One of the most powerful ways I have found to build trust is to ask, "How do you usually approach situations like this?" and then listen. Truly listen. Trust grows when we take the time to understand what matters to someone else and meet them where they are.

Practical takeaway for high-pressure situations

Communicate clearly and honestly - When things go wrong, being open about what happened and focusing on solutions helps rebuild trust faster than blaming others.

Take ownership of your role - Whether you're leading a team or contributing as a colleague, trust grows when people take responsibility and show a willingness to improve.

Lean into strengths - In tense moments, focus on what each person brings to the table. Trust is reinforced when people feel their skills are valued and relied upon.

Practical applications - How to build trust every day,

Trust in daily life shows up in different ways. In teams, it is often built through quiet actions, such as offering help before it is asked for. During our Arctic expedition, stepping in to help someone struggling with their sledge was not dramatic, but it was deeply meaningful. It showed reliability in a way that words never could.

In leadership, trust is cultivated by being transparent about intentions and treating mistakes as learning moments. I once worked with a leader who, after a misstep, invited feedback from the team and owned their role in the situation. That moment did not damage their credibility. It strengthened it.

And when it comes to ourselves, trust begins with the smallest of steps. Moving to England and eventually taking on an international role was a leap, not just of ambition, but of self-belief. I did not need to be fearless. I just needed to act anyway.

Listening

Listening is not just about hearing words. It is about understanding the intent, the emotion, and the meaning beneath them. Trust is built when people feel truly heard, and that requires us to move beyond surface-level listening.

Stephen Covey once said, *"Most people do not listen with the intent to understand; they listen with the intent to reply."* This resonates deeply because many of us wait for our turn to speak, rather than fully engaging with what's being shared. Yet, listening with empathy can transform relationships and deepen trust.

The three levels of listening

- *Surface*
- *Active*
- *Empathetic*

Surface Listening

Listening is one of the most powerful tools for building trust, but not all listening is equal. At the surface level, there's the kind of listening where you're nodding politely, but inside, you're already formulating your reply. I have done this in meetings myself, thinking I understood what someone was saying while really focusing on what I planned to say next. I remember one time when a colleague shared how stressed they were about an upcoming project, and I could tell that they knew I was not fully present. I saw the frustration in their eyes, because I was not truly listening. Looking back, I realise I missed the chance to offer support and instead gave a quick solution that felt rushed.

Active Listening

This is when you repeat or paraphrase what the other person has said, to demonstrate that you're trying to understand. A while ago, I had a team member who was struggling to balance multiple tasks. I said, "So, you're feeling stretched thin because of tight deadlines?" It helped confirm what they were feeling, but I could sense it wasn't quite enough. Something in their expression told me they still felt unseen. I paused, leaned in a little more, and asked, "What part of this is weighing on you the most right now?" That small shift made all the difference. It moved us from surface-level validation into a real conversation. In that moment, I learned that active listening is not just about reflecting back words. It is about staying curious, being willing to go deeper, and showing that you care enough to listen beyond the obvious.

Empathetic Listening

And then, there's empathetic listening. This is where trust deepens, when you listen not just to the words, but to the emotions behind them. I recall a conversation with a team member who confided in me about their insecurities and fear of not belonging. They said, "I just do not feel like I belong here. I keep thinking someone's going to realise I am not cut out for this." I did not jump in with a solution. I paused, looked them in the eye, and said, "That sounds incredibly frustrating. It must be exhausting to feel like you constantly have to prove yourself." In that moment, it was not about solving anything. It was about acknowledging their struggle and making them feel heard. That kind of presence, the ability to connect to what someone is feeling, not just saying, is where trust begins to flourish.

Practical tips for empathetic listening

Practising empathetic listening means going beyond simply hearing words. It starts with giving someone your full attention, removing distractions, and noticing their tone, body language, and pauses. I have learned to listen not just for what someone is saying, but for the emotion behind it.

Asking gentle clarifying questions can deepen the connection. A simple, "When you say X, do you mean Y?" opens up space for better understanding and helps both people feel more aligned.

One thing I have had to work on is resisting the urge to jump in with my own story. Sometimes, we're so eager to show empathy that we interrupt. I have realised the importance of fully absorbing their experience before offering my own.

Assumptions can also quietly distort what we hear. Being aware of my own filters, my cultural background, my beliefs, even my emotional state, helps me stay rooted in the other person's perspective, rather than projecting my own.

And finally, I have learned to be mindful of cultural differences. Some cultures value silence and pauses, while others prefer fast responses and active engagement. Tuning into these differences has helped me build trust and connection more intentionally.

Listening in action - Building trust

I have had moments where I struggled with listening deeply. For instance, I'd hear something that triggered a memory or story of my own, and before I realised it, I had already shifted my focus away from the person speaking. Through practice, I have learned that listening is not about crafting the perfect response. It is about making someone feel truly heard and valued.

When you focus on what's being said, without judgement or interruption, it naturally builds trust and strengthens relationships.

Listening in action - A personal story

When we interviewed a candidate from another country, it was immediately clear that they were knowledgeable and had impressive expertise in their field. However, their strong accent made it difficult for us to fully grasp some of their points. This created a barrier, not because of their ability, but because communication can sometimes get lost in translation.

During the interview, my colleague and I made a conscious effort to practise empathetic listening. Instead of jumping to conclusions or allowing the language barrier to become a hindrance, we asked specific, clarifying questions to ensure we fully understood their perspective. For example, when something was not entirely clear, we would rephrase and confirm: *"Do you mean X, or are you suggesting Y?"*

By creating space for them to express themselves without fear of judgement, we saw their confidence grow as the interview progressed. They began to relax, and their ideas became more detailed and compelling. At the end of the session, they thanked us, saying, *"I have been in interviews where people gave up trying to understand me. You didn't just listen; you made me feel valued."*

That moment stayed with me as a reminder that listening goes far beyond words. It is about making the speaker feel seen, heard, and understood, especially in moments where they may feel vulnerable.

Active listening - More than words

I also experienced the power of listening in a completely different way during a week when I lost my voice. As a speaker and facilitator, I initially felt helpless. How could I connect without words? But in that silence, I discovered something important: trust is not built through conversation alone, it is shaped by how we show up.

Instead of cancelling meetings or stepping back entirely, I found small ways to stay present. I brought a whiteboard with me into in-person meetings, using it to share brief notes or respond silently when needed. I listened with full attention and made space for others to speak, so the absence of my voice did not become a barrier for the conversation to flow. Online, I swapped video calls for written updates or chat messages, choosing my words carefully to ensure they were thoughtful and clear.

Without my voice, I had to tune in differently, noticing tone, body language, and the meaning hidden in pauses. It reminded me of my Arctic expedition, where verbal communication was often impossible. With our faces covered by protective gear and the wind swallowing our voices, we relied on hand signals, eye contact, and mutual intuition to understand one another. A simple glance or nod became a powerful expression of support and understanding.

Both experiences taught me that the deepest form of communication doesn't always come from what we say, but from how we show up. Whether in the workplace, at home, or in the middle of a frozen wilderness, trust is often built through our gestures, our presence, and our ability to truly see and respond to the needs of others.

The art of observation

Observation is about noticing the unspoken, the cues, the silences, and what's left unsaid. During my Arctic expedition, hand signals and eye contact became essential forms of communication because words were rarely an option. In everyday life, this translates to being mindful of subtle gestures, facial expressions, or shifts in energy. Observation builds trust by showing genuine attentiveness to the needs and emotions of others.

Intentional communication

When words are few, they carry more weight. Choosing them with care ensures clarity and impact. This became especially clear in the Arctic, where we often relied on brief hand signals to convey urgency, support, or direction. In daily interactions, pausing before we speak and choosing our words thoughtfully helps ensure that we are not just being heard, but understood.

By combining observation, active listening, and intentional communication, we strengthen our ability to connect meaningfully with others. Trust often resides not in what we say, but in how we make others feel seen, heard, and valued.

Trust as the Foundation

Trust is not just a value. It is a daily practice. Built over time, through care, empathy, and consistency. Whether in the Arctic, the workplace, or at home, it is trust that allows us to connect, collaborate, and grow.

Reflection Prompt

Think back to a time when someone trusted you with something important.

How did that trust make you feel?

What might change if you offered that same trust to someone else or to yourself?

Call to Action

Choose one relationship where trust matters deeply.

Take one small, intentional step today to strengthen it.

That could be listening without interrupting, following through on a promise, or showing vulnerability.

Trust is not built in one moment it grows through the quiet consistency of how we show up.

Final Thought

Trust is not something we're given. It is something we build through presence, through patience, and through the quiet choice to keep showing up.

When I look back on the defining moments of my life from the biting cold of the Arctic, to uncertain beginnings in a new country, to the quiet challenges of leadership each one asked me to trust.

BEYOND THE ICE

Not just in others, but in myself.

Trust that I could move forward without knowing the outcome. That I could rebuild when everything fell apart. That I could belong, even when it didn't feel like I did.

Over time, that trust became my steady anchor. Not loud, but real. Not perfect, but true.

So pause and ask yourself: where in your life does trust need nurturing? And what one small action could you take today to strengthen it?

BEYOND THE ICE

Notes

CHAPTER 7

Connection - The bonds that unite us

"Connection is why we're here; it is what gives purpose and meaning to our lives."- Brené Brown

The power of connection

Connection is the foundation of life. It weaves through our relationships, teams, and communities, shaping our shared experiences and deepening our understanding of one another. But connection does not happen by accident. It is a choice. It grows through intention, effort, and openness. It takes root in vulnerability and is nurtured by the stories we share and the bonds we build.

In this chapter, we will explore how connection is built and strengthened through storytelling. We will walk through moments in the Arctic, the workplace, and our most personal relationships. We will also look at how neuroscience explains the emotional impact of stories, and how storytelling helps build empathy, trust, and belonging across difference. Through shared memory, listening, and openness, we will discover how stories create bridges, and why they matter now more than ever.

Connection is not passive. It is an active force that shapes our personal and professional lives. By understanding the power of storytelling and connection, you will gain tools to deepen relationships, inspire trust, and create meaningful change.

The neuroscience of storytelling

Have you ever been captivated by a story that made you laugh, cry, or reflect deeply? That is not just coincidence. It is science.

When we hear a compelling story, our brains light up. We do not just listen. We feel. This is due to a phenomenon called neural coupling, where the listener's brain begins to mirror the storyteller's. It creates a sense of shared experience, strengthening connection.

Chemicals in the brain also play a role. Dopamine enhances memory and pleasure, helping stories stay with us long after they are told. Oxytocin, sometimes called the "trust hormone," builds empathy and bonding. It is what makes us feel connected not only to the story, but to the person telling it. And cortisol ensures we stay engaged by holding our attention during moments of tension or uncertainty.

Recently, Papa was telling me a story about his best friend Luigi, who he had grown up with as a teenager. Even though it was a memory from over sixty years ago, the way he spoke made it feel like it had happened just yesterday. There was something about the vividness of his voice and the details he shared that brought the past to life in my mind. It was not just the events he was recounting, but the feelings and atmosphere of those moments that came back with such clarity. I felt transported, as if I were walking alongside them sharing their adventures and seeing their bond untold through his eyes.

That is the power of storytelling. It takes us to places and moments we were never part of, yet they feel real because of how the story is shared.

Sometimes, it is not even the words themselves, but the sensory experiences that come with a story that make it feel so vivid. A smell, a sound, or even a familiar sight can pull us back to a specific time in our lives, almost as if we are reliving it. I remember hearing Mamma talk about the town she grew up in, and the way she described the aroma of the local bakery wafting through the streets. That simple mention created a vivid image in my mind, even though I had never walked those streets with her.

It is a phenomenon tied to episodic memory, the part of the brain that allows us to recall specific events, emotions, and sensations from the past. Stories can awaken those memories in ways that make them feel as though they are happening all over again.

Think about the last time you heard a story that truly moved you. Perhaps it was a moment of triumph shared by a friend, or an unexpected turn in someone's journey. That emotional pull was not random. It was your brain forming a connection through trust, empathy, and attention, fuelled by these powerful chemicals. This is why storytelling is so powerful. It goes beyond words, inviting us to see the world through someone else's eyes. Whether it is a tale of resilience or shared joy, stories help us look beyond what separates us and build relationships that stay with us.

BEYOND THE ICE

Arctic - Storytelling in action

In the Arctic, storytelling became the thread that tied us together. After long days trekking across the ice, we would gather in the tent, boots off, jackets unzipped, steam rising from mugs of cocoa clasped tightly in cold hands. There was something sacred about those moments. The stillness outside made our voices feel louder, more deliberate, as if the snow itself was listening.

We did not just recount what we had done. We shared who we were.

Each tent had its own rhythm, its own story. The extreme cold meant we could not always wait for the full team to pack up together, so our journeys each day were often experienced in small clusters. But no matter how scattered we were during the day, we always returned to our tents at night. That reunion with our tent buddy became one of the most grounding parts of the expedition.

Belinda later shared that her tent buddy, Freya, was her "light in the Arctic". She made her laugh every day. Each night, Freya would ask if she had any food in her pockets (as Belinda had a tendency to hide emergency snacks!). She would even frisk her to make sure nothing was smuggled into the sleeping tent (just in case polar bears decided to join.) It became a running joke, but also a nightly ritual that reminded them they were in it together.

In a place so vast and unforgiving, those bonds became everything.

One evening, Amy spoke about the "top twenty reflections" exercise she had done during the day at her tent buddy's suggestion. It was a simple invitation: list twenty thoughts, memories, or moments from your life. But the power came not just in the writing, it came from the sharing.

Her list made us laugh at first. The ache of missing a proper chair. The fantasy of a hot bath. Then it turned. Childhood memories. A heartbreak. A sibling she had not spoken to in years. Her voice softened, and so did the space around us. We leaned in, not out of politeness, but because something real was happening. In the harshest of environments, a crack of vulnerability had opened, and with it, connection rushed in.

That same week, Gaby cried in the tent one evening. Her husband had not sent a message through the satellite phone in days. She tried to brush it off, but we all felt it, that aching quiet when someone you love is just a little too far away. No one tried to fix it. We just let her be. Mandy passed her a piece of chocolate. Someone else made space for her to stretch out her legs. And eventually, Gaby spoke, not about the message, but about what it meant to feel forgotten.

That story stayed with me. Not because of the tears, but because of how we responded. No one tried to fill the silence or offer a silver lining. We met her where she was.

The satellite phone moment reminded me of something from when I was eleven, on a school ski trip in the mountains. For three weeks, we skied in the afternoons and studied in the mornings. It was my first time away from home for so long. Families sent letters during our time away, some filled with joyful updates, others with gentle reminders of home, or even a few coins tucked inside as treats. But I also remember the children who waited for letters that never arrived. That quiet kind of heartbreak still lingers with me.

In the Arctic, we were each handed a letter too. But this time, it was unexpected. Without our knowing, our loved ones had been asked to write messages of encouragement before the expedition began. The timing could not have been more perfect. The cold had started to seep deeper. Fatigue was etched into our faces. Morale was thinning.

I remember holding the envelope, puzzled at first, unsure what it contained. When I opened it and recognised the handwriting, my breath caught. The words reached straight into the ache I had been carrying but had not named. One friend whispered through tears, "I had no idea he thought this about me." Another sat silently, rereading her letter over and over, the raw cold momentarily replaced by warmth.

That small gesture was more than a morale boost. It was a reminder that we were held, seen, and remembered, even from afar. In a place where everything felt stripped down to survival, those letters brought us back to something deeply human.

Just like a well-told story, they connected us, not only to the people who wrote them, but to one another. They reminded us of who we were beyond the expedition. And they reminded me that connection, when rooted in care and surprise, can reach us even in the harshest conditions.

Storytelling across cultures - When stories transcend language

In one of my global workshops, I opened with a personal story about navigating conflicting expectations in corporate life. I did not begin with a slide deck. I began with my voice.

After the session, participants from different cultural backgrounds came forward. Not to ask about my credentials, but to share their own stories. That is the power of storytelling. It builds trust and connection, even when language, culture, and life experiences differ.

In the workplace, storytelling can inspire trust, create a sense of belonging, and even help resolve conflict. I remember working with a leader who began a strategy meeting by speaking openly about his self-doubt. He said, "I have been in this role for years, but there are still moments I walk into meetings and wonder if I am enough."

The shift in the room was immediate. Team members, previously quiet, began opening up. Some shared fears about new responsibilities, others admitted to feeling overwhelmed or disconnected. What began as a business discussion became something more human.

But it was not just the story. It was what happened next. That same leader began following up with regular one-to-one check-ins. He shared his own reflections in team newsletters and created space for others to do the same. His vulnerability was not a one-time event. It became a practice. And over time, that team became one of the most collaborative and high-performing groups I have worked with. It all started with a story.

In another meeting, with a global client team, I watched a room grow tense as misunderstandings began to surface. Everyone was trying to contribute, but different communication styles created friction. I sensed the frustration building. So, I paused and shared a story. I spoke about a time when I led a multicultural team and struggled to find common ground. I shared what I learned: to slow down, to listen differently, and to adapt.

That one story shifted the energy. One participant said, "I felt like no one understood me. But now I think we can get there." Others began sharing their concerns and hopes more freely. It was not the story alone that made the difference. It was the invitation it created. A way back to connection.

In yet another setting, I opened a keynote with a story of early failure and resilience. It was a room full of international leaders, many of whom I had never met. But as I spoke about learning to navigate different viewpoints and build trust across teams, I saw heads nodding. People leaned in. Afterward, several came up to say, "That could have been my story."

That is what storytelling does. It reminds us that beneath all our differences, we share emotions, challenges, and values. We connect not just through facts, but through moments that feel familiar, even if our lives are not.

BEYOND THE ICE

Storytelling is not just about self-expression. It is a way to create space where others feel recognised, included, and understood. When we share stories that reflect our values or challenges, we invite others to connect with us in a more human way. Whether in personal conversations or professional settings, this kind of openness builds a sense of shared humanity.

Here are five ways to use storytelling to build connection

Start with emotion - Use stories that tap into feelings we all recognise, such as joy, fear, hope, or longing.

Be real - Share experiences that are honest and personal. Authentic stories carry more weight than perfect ones.

Use sensory detail - Help people see, feel, or imagine the moment by describing small but vivid details.

Connect the story to meaning - Explain why the story matters. Link it to a value, lesson, or shift in perspective.

Leave space for others - A powerful story is not about impressing others. It is about making space for someone else to be seen and heard.

Storytelling in personal connection

Connection begins at home. It is easy to assume that the people closest to us know us well, but even in the most familiar relationships, storytelling can deepen bonds in profound ways.

BEYOND THE ICE

Personal story - A connection that crosses generations

I remember a moment with my son when he was preparing to transition to university. As we packed his belongings and prepared for this new chapter, I could see the excitement in his eyes, a mixture of anticipation and eagerness to embrace his independence. Watching him, I felt a deep mix of pride and nostalgia, and I decided to share a piece of my own story with him. I told him about the day I left France to move to England alone, with nothing more than a heart full of determination. I shared how excited I was to finally claim my freedom and start a life on my own terms. I was ready to leave, even though I knew I would miss my two closest friends. But even amidst the excitement, my departure was tinged with a bittersweet sadness. No one had hugged me goodbye. No one had wished me luck or given me anything to remember them by. It felt as though no one truly believed I would succeed. It was as if my journey was not real to anyone but me.

For him, I wanted things to be different. As a family, we prepared a small hamper filled with personalised items, each one carrying a memory or a meaning he could hold onto whenever he needed a reminder of home. The final gift in the hamper was a custom-made jigsaw piece, engraved with the words: "You are our missing piece." As we handed it to him, we said, "This completes the picture, because without you, nothing quite fits."

It was not just a keepsake; it was a symbol of belonging, a reminder that no matter how far he went, he would always have a place where he was valued, seen, and deeply loved.

As I shared my story, I saw his shoulders relax and his smile soften. It was not just a moment of comfort; it was a bridge to a deeper connection. By the end of our conversation, he opened up about his own mix of emotions, the thrill of starting this new chapter, the fear of the unknown, and the sadness of leaving familiar faces behind.

That day, I learned once again that storytelling is not just about recounting the past. It is a way to build trust, to create space for vulnerability, and to remind the people we love that they are never truly alone. It is in those moments, whether shared through words, actions, or gestures, that connection takes root and grows stronger. Letting him go was bittersweet, but sharing my own story made me realise that connection is not about holding on; it is about giving others the tools to thrive on their own, knowing they always have a place to return to.

And here's something I have learned over the years; if we do not listen to the "little things"- those moments that might seem trivial to us but are huge to someone else - we will never hear the big things later on. It is easy to dismiss those "small dramas," especially when they seem insignificant in our adult lives. But in those moments, for others, that is everything. When we listen, truly listen, to the everyday struggles, we create a space where deeper connections can grow. Listening is not just for the important conversations; it is in these small moments where we build trust and understanding.

Since my son left for university, our family dynamic has naturally shifted, and we no longer share the small, everyday moments as we used to. To stay connected, we started a simple tradition at the end of each week: we share photos that made an impact on us. Each of us selects images from our weekly download that captured something meaningful, whether they made us laugh, cry, cringe, or reflect on our week. Some photos need explanations, sparking stories and conversations, while others speak for themselves, bringing a smile to our faces. My daughter often adds a song that resonated with her during the week, creating an emotional link that ties us together despite the miles. it is a way to stay present in each other's lives and share the moments that shaped us, no matter how big or small.

Storytelling takes many forms: sometimes through a glance, a hug, or even a kiss. These simple gestures often convey more than words ever could, reminding us that connection is not just about sharing stories but about being present in the ways that matter most.

Finding connection in difference

Connection is not always found in familiar places; it often thrives when we step outside our comfort zones. When I first moved to England, I made a deliberate choice - I didn't want to surround myself with French people. Some might ask why, but for me, the answer was clear. I had chosen this journey to immerse myself in a different culture, to learn a new language, and to experience life in a way that couldn't happen if I stayed in a familiar bubble. I thought, *"If I spend my time with French speakers, I might as well have stayed home."*

Instead, I sought out opportunities to connect with people who were different from me. I relished the challenge of speaking English, discovering expressions and idioms that carried meanings far removed from their French equivalents. It was like unlocking a new way of seeing the world. That curiosity about difference hasn't left me, it is something I carry with me even today.

Of course, over the years, I have rekindled connections with French people living in Britain (*especially those who've made a huge effort to anglicise, often in the most endearing ways*). Hearing their unique stories is always fascinating, as it highlights the different ways people adapt and weave their identity between two cultures.

Stepping into someone else's world for a moment...

Recently, I finally had the chance to attend a Human Library, something I first heard about three years ago but had never managed to experience until now.

For those unfamiliar, The Human Library® is exactly what it sounds like - a library of people. But instead of borrowing books, you "borrow" a conversation. Each book is a person who has volunteered to share their lived experiences, creating a safe space for open dialogue that challenges stigma and stereotypes.

I walked in with curiosity. I left with perspective.

There were books covering all sorts of topics: mental health, transgender identity, organ transplants, addiction, suicide, and many more. Some topics were ones I could empathise with, while others were far outside my own lived experience. But here's what struck me: sometimes, we hesitate to approach certain stories because we fear what they might reflect back on us.

It is easy to think we are far removed from certain struggles, addiction, for instance, but listening to these conversations made me realise how many of us live with habits, behaviours, or coping mechanisms that aren't so different.

We often associate addiction with things like alcohol or drugs, but it is not always the obvious. It can also show up in everyday habits:

The bar of chocolate you reach for without thinking.

The instant gratification of an online purchase.

The rush of getting another tattoo.

While these may not carry the same consequences, they remind us how human it is to seek comfort, escape, or control in different ways.

Challenging our own assumptions

The visit to the Human Library reminded me of an essential truth: understanding begins when we stop assuming. It is easy to think we already know someone's story based on appearances, job titles, or a single detail from their past. But real connection happens when we take the time to ask, listen, and truly see beyond the surface.

There are many ways to expand your perspective, but it often begins with self-awareness. One powerful tool is the free and anonymous Implicit Association Test from Harvard, designed to reveal the hidden biases we all carry. It is not about blame; it is about recognising the filters through which we see the world. (You can explore it at *projectimplicit.net*.)

Another way is by actively seeking out real stories. Whether through initiatives like the Human Library, through books, podcasts, or conversations, immersing yourself in perspectives that differ from your own can shift your understanding in profound ways. Sometimes, all it takes is pausing before a snap judgement, catching yourself in the moment and asking, *"Am I seeing the full picture?"*

If you ever get the chance to attend a Human Library, I encourage you to go. Not just to hear someone else's story, but to reflect on your own. The experience will likely stay with you long after the conversation ends.

So, ask yourself, when was the last time you actively sought out someone with a different perspective? How did it change the way you saw the world?

Reflecting on our own stories can be a powerful way to build connection. Think about a story that shaped who you are, who would benefit from hearing it, and why? Consider the last time you shared a personal story in a professional setting. How did it change the tone of the conversation or shift the connection in the room?

You might also recall a moment when someone else's story changed your perspective or helped you see them

BEYOND THE ICE

more clearly. What was it about their story that stayed with you? If you lead a team, how might you use storytelling to build trust and bring people closer together?

Take five minutes to identify a story that reflects your values or shows your resilience. Write it down, and consider where it might be shared, in a conversation, a meeting, or even a quiet one-to-one. The next time you lead a group or facilitate a discussion, consider beginning with a short personal story that reflects the theme. Notice how it changes the dynamic and creates space for others to open up.

And finally, stay curious. Invite a colleague, friend, or family member to share a story that shaped them and listen without interrupting. You might be surprised by what you learn and how it changes your understanding of them.

Before your next presentation or conversation, think about a story that highlights a key value, lesson, or experience relevant to your audience. Ask yourself:

"How can this story make my message more relatable, human, and memorable?"

Choose one that resonates with the challenges or aspirations of your audience to bridge gaps, cultivate understanding, and inspire action.

Reflection Prompt

Recall a story that shifted your understanding of someone.

What made it so powerful?

Now think about someone you know well but whose deeper story you have never really heard.

What might open that door?

Call to Action

Connection is not a single moment. It is a series of choices to see, hear, and value others. Whether through storytelling, empathy, or curiosity, every act of connection brings us closer to understanding what it means to be human.

This week, take five minutes to reflect on a story from your life that reveals something important about who you are or what you value.

Write it down. Consider where it might be shared—with a colleague, a friend, or a loved one.

Then, make space for someone else. Invite them to share a story that shaped them.

Listen not just to their words, but to what matters underneath.

Stories build trust. They create bridges. And every time we share one with honesty, we invite connection to deepen.

Final Thought

Connection is rarely built in the spotlight.

It lives in quiet moments, when we choose to stay, to listen, to care.

The stories we share and the way we receive the stories of others shape the fabric of our relationships.

In the end, it is not perfection that connects us. It is truth.

So pause. Be present. Share something real. And in doing so, you might just build a bridge that lasts a lifetime.

Notes

BEYOND THE ICE

CHAPTER 8

Leadership - Inspiring others through action

"Leadership is not about titles or flowcharts. It is about one life influencing another."
John C. Maxwell

Redefining leadership

Leadership rises above roles or authority. It is shaped by what we do, why we do it, and how we lift others in the process. True leaders cultivate trust, embrace vulnerability, and inspire those around them to reach their potential. They create environments where individuals feel valued, included, and motivated to contribute their best.

In this chapter, we will explore leadership through three distinct yet interconnected lenses. First, we will step into the harsh conditions of the Arctic, where leadership was tested and defined by resilience, unity, and adaptability. Then we will move into the business world, where effective leadership is grounded in empathy, authenticity, and inclusion. Finally, we will reflect on what it means to lead ourselves – to act with integrity, face fear, and grow through vulnerability.

Arctic - Leadership in action

Creating unity in crisis

In extreme environments, every small action can mean the difference between success and failure. True leadership often emerges in moments of quiet strength and collaboration. During a white blizzard in the Arctic, visibility dropped to zero, and the howling wind and sharp cold made every step a challenge. Our guide gathered us to discuss whether to proceed or wait. Instead of dictating the decision, they invited us to share our perspectives. We stopped, pulled out the map, and considered alternative routes. Staying put was not an option; it was too risky to wait for the weather to improve. To my surprise, people who rarely spoke during the expedition began contributing thoughtful input, weighing the risks of each option. That act of inclusion brought a fresh sense of unity and demonstrated that leadership is about collective strength, especially in moments of crisis.

Flattening hierarchies in extreme conditions

In the Arctic, roles did not matter. Directors and juniors alike had to pitch tents, melt ice, and pull sleds. It was the ultimate leveller. We quickly realised that flexibility was essential. Everyone had to pitch in, regardless of title or experience. Sharing responsibility became essential not just for meeting the demands of the expedition, but for sustaining morale and fairness. Leadership revealed itself through those who took initiative and cared for others.

Adapting to new realities together

Perseverance required collective effort and constant adaptability. Every day brought fresh challenges, from managing unpredictable terrain to coping with fatigue. We relied on shared responsibilities, effective communication, and mutual trust to overcome these hurdles.

Each day in the Arctic, completing the trek was not just a physical necessity, it was a quiet exercise in mutual trust. Every step forward depended on our belief in one another's strength and commitment. As exhaustion built and tempers occasionally frayed, it became clear that fairness in how we shared the load mattered. One evening, Amy suggested rotating tasks to prevent anyone from being stuck with the more demanding or thankless roles. It was a small proposal, but its impact was immediate and lasting. The atmosphere shifted. People felt seen and valued. In those moments, we relied not on commands or authority, but on kindness, unspoken cues, and shared understanding. Leadership emerged through presence, respect, and an unwavering commitment to the well-being of the group.

Key moment of reflection - Small details matter

Leadership in the Arctic was not about loud proclamations but noticing small details that kept the team moving forward. For example, when melting ice for drinking water, starting with a bit of liquid water in the pot prevented burning the ice. Missing this step could ruin our only source of hydration, it was a small but vital action that kept us going.

Lesson: Inclusive leadership is not about hierarchy; it is about creating environments where everyone feels empowered to contribute.

Practical Takeaways

In high-pressure situations, I have found that pausing to involve the team in decision-making builds not just trust, but a shared sense of ownership. It is through these moments of collaboration that people feel valued and heard. Likewise, noticing the small details, whether it is checking in on someone who seems quiet or adjusting a process that is not working, can be the glue that holds a team together. These seemingly minor choices become powerful acts of leadership when they're grounded in care and attentiveness.

Leadership Frameworks - Guiding core principles in action

Leadership is not one-size-fits-all. Different models offer valuable insights, depending on the situation. Here are two frameworks that resonate deeply with my journey:

1. Servant Leadership - Empowering through support

Servant leadership is grounded in the belief that a leader's role is to support and elevate others. I saw this in action during the Arctic trek when one of us reached a breaking point, physically drained and considering whether to return to base camp. Our guide noticed and made the deliberate choice to pause the group, even though we were on a tight schedule. Rather than making a public announcement or drawing attention to her struggle, she took her aside and listened quietly, without judgement. Afterwards, she gently encouraged the rest of us to support her in small, non-intrusive ways, making sure she felt carried - not singled out.

It was a subtle moment of leadership, but one that reminded me how powerfully compassion can build resilience.

2. Adaptive Leadership

During a major corporate restructure, I observed a leader who embodied adaptive leadership. She acknowledged the uncertainty head-on, while reinforcing a hopeful vision of what was possible. When the team needed direction, she offered clear, practical guidance. When morale dipped, she led with empathy, listening to concerns and validating emotions without sugarcoating the reality.

Her ability to adjust her approach based on what the team needed in each moment built deep trust and allowed the group to move forward with renewed confidence.

Why these models matter

Both frameworks align with the belief that leadership is about connection, adaptability, and empowerment. Whether guiding a team through an Arctic blizzard or managing cultural differences in a global project, these core principles have consistently proven invaluable.

Lesson: Effective leadership adapts to the moment while remaining rooted in empowering others. By understanding and applying frameworks like servant and adaptive leadership, leaders can overcome challenges with greater empathy and effectiveness.

Practical Takeaways

As I reflect on my own leadership journey, I often ask myself whether I am creating the conditions for others to grow. Am I showing up in a way that puts their development at the heart of what I do? Being adaptable means listening deeply to what my team needs in a given moment, sometimes it is guidance, other times it is simply being a steady presence. I try to lead by building trust slowly and consistently, creating real opportunities for contribution and ownership. That, for me, is the essence of servant leadership.

Analogies that bring leadership to life

Leadership can often feel abstract. But sometimes, it takes a simple image - a fire, a compass, a tent in a storm - to reveal what it really means in practice. Here are three ways leadership mirrors resilience in the Arctic:

"Leadership is like building a fire in the Arctic."

You begin with the right materials: dry wood, kindling, and a clear understanding of your surroundings. In the same way, great leaders recognise and harness the strengths of their team, knowing what each person brings to the flame. But starting a fire is only the beginning. It takes thoughtful preparation to ensure it lasts. A poorly built fire fizzles out quickly, just as a team without a clear structure or purpose can lose its way. And even the strongest fire requires tending. Leadership, too, demands ongoing care, consistent communication, and a reliable presence that keeps the warmth alive through challenges.

"Leadership is like using a compass in a snowstorm."

In blinding conditions, when visibility drops to near zero, that compass becomes your only guide. A strong leader must know their core values and purpose and use them to stay oriented in uncertain terrain. But knowing the destination is not enough. Leaders must be willing to adjust their path when the route becomes impassable, staying adaptable without losing sight of the goal. Just as we trusted our compass, teams need to trust that their leader's judgement is grounded in clarity, not control.

"Leadership is like pitching a tent in a storm."

The winds whip around you, the ground is unstable, and the pressure to protect everyone is intense. A tent needs strong pegs to stand firm, just like a team needs trust to stay together when the pressure rises. It also needs space for everyone. Inclusive leadership means making sure every voice has room to be heard, every person feels safe, and no one is left outside. And just like setting up camp, leadership is not a solo act. The best leaders do not build alone. They guide others to contribute, to hold the corners, to create a shared shelter in uncertain times.

Leadership in business - Leading with empathy and vision

In global teams, cultural expectations can vary widely. Clarity, open discussion, and curiosity are essential for building shared understanding and trust.

Empathy builds psychological safety, especially during periods of change. I recall a time when, after ten years with a company, we were informed of a decision to relocate the office two hours away. At that point in my life, I had small children, and the prospect of extended daily commutes was daunting.

The leader, tasked with delivering this news, did not have a polished speech or all the answers. Instead, she spoke from the heart, acknowledged the challenge, and promised to support us through the transition. Her honesty and genuine concern created a space where we felt seen and supported, even amidst uncertainty.

This experience reinforced that leadership is not about having all the answers. It is about creating an environment where people feel heard, valued, and empowered. By approaching the situation with sincerity and openness, our leader fostered trust and resilience within the team.

Lesson: Leadership is not about having all the answers. It is about creating trust through empathy, clarity, and openness, especially in times of uncertainty.

Practical Takeaways

In my experience, psychological safety doesn't come from policy, it comes from presence. It starts when leaders are willing to be vulnerable, to admit what they do not know, and to create space for others to do the same. I have learned to seek out the diverse perspectives on my team, not just as a box-ticking exercise, but because those differences are the source of better decisions and stronger outcomes. Sometimes it is data that opens the door, but more often, it is stories, real, human examples, that connect people to a bigger purpose and encourage inclusive leadership that truly works.

Addressing difficult conversations

Difficult conversations are inevitable as a leader, whether it is providing constructive feedback, supporting people through transitions, or resolving team conflicts. The key to handling these situations effectively is combining empathy with clarity.

For example, when delivering tough news, start by stating the impact: "This decision affects the team deeply, and here is how I am addressing it with fairness and transparency."

Acknowledging emotions creates space for trust, while providing clear next steps ensures that your team understands the way forward. When leaders approach these conversations with compassion and honesty, they reinforce their commitment to their team's well-being, even in challenging times.

Actionable advice

Leading through difficulty means starting with empathy, acknowledging the very real emotions in the room, and then moving forward with clarity. I once worked on a meaningful project with a company focused on becoming a more inclusive and connected workplace. We had built trust, met regularly, and made real progress, until an unexpected industry downturn cut their budget by nearly a quarter.

I had to deliver the news to the group. The disappointment in the room was palpable, especially for those who had seen similar efforts fade in the past. I paused, acknowledged the shift, and asked one simple question, "What still matters most?"

Their answers were clear. They did not ask for more resources or new plans. They wanted to keep learning, stay connected, and ensure the work was seen through. So we adapted. We reshaped the final phase to focus on what felt essential. It became less about scope and more about intention, and the impact, in the end, was deeper because it was co-created.

Cultural differences can create distance if we ignore them, but they can also become a bridge when we name them, share our own learning, and invite others to do the same. In times of uncertainty, I try to stay grounded in honesty and keep returning to the shared vision that holds us together. That is what keeps teams engaged when the path is unclear.

Personal Leadership - Leading yourself first

Stepping away from stability

Leadership is not just about guiding teams; it is about guiding yourself first. Before I could lead others with confidence, I had to build that confidence within myself. Leaving the stability of my corporate career to start my own business was a leap of faith. It required courage, vulnerability, and a deep alignment with my values. That decision not only reshaped my life but also inspired those around me to pursue paths that resonated with their truths.

Self-Awareness as a catalyst for growth

Personal growth is the foundation of effective leadership. As leaders, we must first understand ourselves - our values, strengths, and blind spots - before we can guide others. One of my most transformative experiences in this regard came when I transitioned from a corporate career to becoming a facilitator.

In the early days of this shift, I realised I often avoided conflict to keep the peace, but this sometimes prevented resolution and growth. While this worked in some scenarios, I noticed it sometimes led to unresolved issues or missed opportunities for growth. Through self-reflection and feedback, I learned that addressing difficult conversations directly, while maintaining empathy, was the most effective approach. For example, during a workshop, a participant challenged my methodology. Instead of sidestepping the issue, I paused to listen and engaged in an open discussion. Not only did this strengthen my credibility, but it also created trust and respect within the group.

Finding the courage to lead authentically

Starting my business meant facing fears I'd buried deep. Letting go of corporate stability was not just a career decision; it was a personal reckoning. I had to trust my instincts, lead myself, and believe that the value I bring lies not in conformity but in authenticity. By aligning my actions with my values of authenticity and empowerment, I found the courage to take this leap. The process was not just about building a business; it was about rediscovering and believing in myself through self- leadership.

Believing in the potential of others

One of the greatest lessons I have learned as a leader is the power of believing in others. Whether coaching a team member or guiding a workshop participant, I have always had an innate ability to see their potential, even when they couldn't see it themselves. I once mentored a consultant who was hesitant about stepping into a leadership role. By providing encouragement and a safe space to test their skills, I helped them find the confidence to lead effectively. Watching them thrive only reinforced my belief that leadership is about empowering others to overcome their doubts and realise their capabilities.

Lesson: Personal growth translates directly to stronger leadership. When leaders are self-aware and authentic, they inspire trust, confidence, and growth in those around them.

Practical Takeaways

Reflect on your leadership style and identify areas where personal growth can help you lead more intentionally. Personal growth is central to the way I lead. I often reflect on where I might be getting in my own way, what habits, assumptions, or blind spots I need to confront in order to grow. Asking for feedback has been one of the most humbling and rewarding practices, not just from clients or senior leaders, but from peers and those I work with every day. I have also learned to use my own experiences, not as a script, but as a connection point. By sharing where I have stumbled and how I have learned, I have seen others begin to believe more deeply in their own ability to lead.

Personal Example - Owning my self-doubt

When I transitioned from corporate life to becoming a facilitator and coach, I often doubted my ability to succeed. Rather than hiding my insecurities, I shared them with peers and mentors. To my surprise, this honesty did not weaken their respect, it deepened it. They shared their own stories of imposter syndrome, and their support became a catalyst for my growth.

As a facilitator, I have found that being open about my vulnerabilities helps participants connect with me on a deeper level. It shows them that leadership is not about being perfect, it is about being authentic. I do not claim to know it all, but by sharing my experiences and expertise, I invite others to learn from my journey, and from my mistakes. (After all, we do not grow old enough to make them all ourselves!)

Lesson: Vulnerability is a pathway that connects leaders to their teams. It builds relatability and inspires others to embrace their imperfections.

Practical takeaways for leaders

The first time I shared a personal story in a team meeting, I was not sure how it would land. But almost immediately, I saw the shift, it softened the space, made others feel safer, and encouraged more honest dialogue. Since then, I have made it a habit. And when I get things wrong, (which we all do) I name it openly, not just to clear the air, but to model what resilience really looks like in practice. It is never about being flawless. It is about being real.

Lessons from observing poor leadership

Great leaders inspire us, but poor leadership leaves equally lasting lessons. Reflecting on examples of ineffective leadership can reveal what not to do and reinforce the importance of leading with integrity, empathy, and accountability.

Avoiding Accountability - The ripple effect of inaction

During my corporate career, I worked under a leader who consistently avoided accountability during crises. When a major client raised concerns about project delays, instead of addressing the issue head-on, the leader deflected responsibility to others in the team.

This lack of ownership created confusion and resentment, ultimately eroding trust and morale.

This taught me that leadership is not about perfection; it is about standing firm, owning mistakes, and making tough decisions. When leaders avoid accountability, they fail to meet their teams' expectations and lose credibility. Authentic leadership requires acknowledging challenges and taking clear, decisive action, even when it is uncomfortable.

Favouritism and ignoring feedback can quietly undermine trust. In contrast, leaders who celebrate diverse contributions and actively seek input create environments where teams feel valued and encouraged to innovate.

Practical Takeaway

Looking back, some of the most respected leaders I have worked with weren't those who never made mistakes, they were the ones who admitted them with grace. They owned their choices, invited dialogue, and showed us that accountability was not optional. I have also seen how quietly harmful it can be when opportunities aren't distributed fairly. If some voices are always louder or more rewarded, others shrink. I now make it a point to examine how work is shared and who gets recognised. Feedback, too, is a gift - one we often avoid but so desperately need. Creating honest spaces to hear it and act on it has transformed the way I lead.

Practical strategies for inclusive leadership:

Facilitate and Empower - Leadership is about stepping into the circle, not standing at the top of a pyramid. Empower your team by facilitating collaboration and valuing their unique contributions. Recognise that diversity is not just about representation, it is about leveraging differences to drive innovation and create solutions that resonate with real people.

Encourage Ownership - Delegate tasks thoughtfully and ensure everyone feels their contributions matter. Share decision-making responsibilities and encourage input from quieter voices to cultivate engagement and trust.

Leadership exercises and tools - Practical steps for growth

Leadership is not just about understanding core principles, it is about putting them into practice. Here are actionable tools and exercises to help you and your team grow:

One of the most powerful exercises I have used to build empathy within teams involves something I call a "perspective swap." In a meeting, I'll invite each person to share a recent decision they've made (whether big or small) and explain their reasoning behind it. As each story unfolds, the group begins to recognise how varied our thinking can be, and how those differences are a strength, not a threat. These reflections often lead to deeper insights about how diversity of thought helps shape better decisions. Over time, this kind of open sharing builds mutual respect and appreciation for perspectives that may otherwise go unnoticed.

Another tool that has proven incredibly valuable is creating space for feedback circles. In these sessions, team members come together with the shared purpose of growing, not through formal reviews, but through open and honest dialogue. We begin by setting intentions; feedback should be specific, focused on behaviours, and always delivered with the goal of building each other up. People are encouraged to name something they appreciate about a colleague, and then gently offer one suggestion for growth. The result? A culture where feedback becomes normal, not feared. Where trust is built through honesty, and where learning is a shared endeavour.

Language shapes our reality, and I have found that small shifts in the words we choose can have a big impact on how included people feel. To explore this, I have guided teams through what I call an "inclusive language reflection." We start by looking at everyday phrases, the ones we might say without thinking, that can unintentionally exclude or stereotype. Then, together, we explore alternatives and share experiences of how language has affected us. Over the weeks that follow, people begin to notice their words more carefully, often catching themselves mid-sentence and adjusting in real time. It is a gentle but powerful way to build awareness and make inclusion part of the everyday conversation.

When I reflect on what it means to lead inclusively, I often begin with small, actionable intentions. What's one meaningful change I can make this week to help someone feel more included, more heard? These changes do not need to be dramatic, they often start with how we listen, how we create space in conversations, or how we invite quieter voices into the conversation. I also think back to moments when I have felt excluded. How did that affect my confidence or performance? What assumptions were made about me, and how might I ensure others never feel the same under my leadership?

Empathy is another cornerstone. I try to revisit recent decisions and ask myself whose perspective was missing. Did I truly listen to the range of experiences in the room? Was I open to seeing things in a new way? Growth, I have learned, also comes through feedback. Some of the hardest things I have heard have been the ones that helped me grow the most. I reflect on what feedback has resonated and how I have responded to it over time.

And perhaps the most important reflection of all: What impact do I want my leadership to have on others? Not just in terms of goals and deliverables, but in how they feel, how they grow, and how they lead others in turn.

BEYOND THE ICE

Bringing people together - A Legacy beyond ourselves

Some of the most powerful acts of leadership happen far from boardrooms and presentations. One of the moments I am proudest of took place not during a strategy meeting, but on a muddy patch of earth in a hospital garden. At the company where I worked, we were given two days each year to support a cause of our choice. Many spent those days painting school walls or volunteering in food banks. But I wanted to do something that would connect us, not just to a task, but to each other, to the community, and to something meaningful.

I organised a day in the garden of a local hospital, a space that had once been lovingly tended by a woman who had passed away the year before. She had cared for it quietly, without fanfare, creating a small sanctuary of peace for patients and visitors alike. With her gone, the garden had been neglected. I saw an opportunity not only to restore it, but to honour her spirit.

In the weeks leading up to our community day, we held a bake sale at the office. Everyone contributed. Even those who could not attend helped by baking, donating, or buying. On the day itself, we dug, weeded, planted, and worked shoulder to shoulder. We sweated, laughed, and dug deep, not just into the earth, but into ourselves. But the most meaningful moment came at the end. With the funds we had raised, we commissioned a plaque in her memory. When we unveiled it, her grown children were there, standing in the very garden their mother had once tended with quiet devotion.

That day, we did more than clear weeds or plant flowers. We restored a legacy. We created connection. And we laid the foundation for something that would last.

What I remember most was the stillness. As the plaque was revealed, everyone stood in silence. Not because they had to, but because they understood. Leadership, I realised then, is not about orchestrating dramatic displays. It is about bringing people together to create something that matters. Something lasting. Something rooted in care and intention.

The leadership journey

As I look back on my leadership journey, from the biting winds of the Arctic to the shifting landscapes of corporate life, I return to one pivotal moment. It was the final day of our Arctic expedition. We were tired, sore, and weather-beaten. Each step felt heavier than the last. And then, something extraordinary happened. Without a word, we instinctively reached out and linked arms, one by one, shoulder to shoulder. We walked the last stretch as one team. Not out of necessity, but out of something deeper - trust.

In that moment, I understood what leadership truly meant. It was not about being first. It was not about being the loudest or the most confident. It was about making sure no one was left behind. It was about recognising when someone needed support. And it was about quietly believing in others, even when they doubted themselves.

That final act of linking arms was more than a gesture of solidarity. It reflected how far we had come, not only across the Arctic but within ourselves. We had started as individuals, carrying our own fears and fatigue. We finished as a team, each one of us becoming the reason another kept going.

Because true leadership is not about reaching the summit first. It is about walking together, through storms, across crevasses, into uncertainty, and helping others believe they can make it too.

Leadership is about seeing potential where others see limitations. It is about extending support where others hesitate. And it is about inspiring courage where doubt once stood.

Reflection Prompt

Think about a moment when someone's leadership made you feel seen, valued, or inspired.

What did they do that left a lasting impression?

Now ask yourself: how might you lead in that same spirit today?

Call to Action

Leadership is not a title. It is a choice we make each day, in how we show up, how we listen, and how we lift others.

Take a moment to reflect on how you lead in your everyday life whether in a meeting, a conversation, or a quiet moment of support.

Think about the last time you created space for someone else to speak. Or a moment when you recognised a strength in someone that they had not yet seen in themselves.

These small moments matter. They build trust. They build confidence. They build momentum.

You do not need permission to lead. You only need presence, intention, and care.

Final Thought

Leadership is not reserved for titles or positions.

BEYOND THE ICE

It lives in how we show up, how we listen, and how we hold space for others to grow.

The most impactful leaders are often the quiet ones, the steady ones, the ones who lead by example.

So, as you move forward, ask yourself:

What kind of leader do you want to be when no one is watching?

BEYOND THE ICE

Notes

CHAPTER 9

Diversity - Strengthening our differences

"It is not our differences that divide us. It is our inability to recognize, accept, and celebrate those differences."- Audre Lorde

In this chapter, we will explore how diversity runs far deeper than what we can see on the surface. It is shaped by background, personality, experience, and countless invisible factors. We will reflect on how our lived experiences influence the way we lead, connect, and find belonging. And we will see how embracing difference, rather than managing it, creates stronger, more resilient, and more innovative teams.

We will reflect on stories from my childhood, the Arctic, and the workplace to explore what true inclusion looks like and how each of us can create environments where everyone is seen, valued, and heard.

Struggling with identity

It was the third time that week that I got up after being pushed down on the street, spat at, and called a 'nigger.' I slowly got back up, dusted myself off, and kept walking to school. I was used to it by now, mentally armed and ready to face the world. In a world where I was constantly reminded that I was different, it was not just a word, it was a message that I did not belong.

I was a child, but I already understood that my skin colour meant something to others before I even had the words to describe it. I did not know why it made them look at me with hostility or why my existence seemed to provoke anger. But I knew one thing - I was not like everyone else, and that made life harder.

When you just want to belong

At school, I learned that silence was a form of survival. No one talked to me about what was happening, certainly not my teachers. They kept their distance, unsure of what to say, they saw me as different in a way that made them uncomfortable.

I didn't want to be a problem. I didn't want to 'disturb' anyone with my feelings. So, I became the clown. If I could make people laugh, maybe they would forget I was not like them. If I could distract them, perhaps they would see me as just another kid, not an outsider. I never really knew whether they laughed with me or at me. But I started performing, smiling when I did not feel like it, pretending that nothing hurt, even when it did.

However, the silence came at a cost. I began to believe that I was not good enough, that I would never be accepted, and that I would never succeed.

I so desperately wanted to change, to look like my family, my classmates, the people who belonged. I remember standing in front of the mirror, scratching at my skin until it turned red, hoping that underneath, I would find a sense of acceptance. I thought that if I could just change, if I could just blend in, everything would be easier.

The reminders of my difference came from everywhere, even my own home. I remember the day I brought home my class photo, eager to show it to my family. My brother took one look at it and laughed, pointing at the image; "That photo is not right, there's a black dot on it." I looked at the picture, confused, searching for the flaw he was talking about. Then I realised. He meant me. I laughed along, pretending it didn't matter, pretending I understood the joke. But something shifted inside me that day. I understood, with more clarity than ever before, that no matter how hard I tried, I would never blend in.

One day, I overheard someone talking about skin-lightening cream. I did not understand how it worked, but I knew what it promised; a chance to be normal. I never had access to it, but I know that if I had, I would have tried it without hesitation. Just the thought that something could erase the part of me that made my life so difficult was enough to keep me awake at night. I did not want to stand out, I just wanted to exist without feeling like I had to fight for my place in the world.

Personal lesson

For years, I believed my difference was a burden. But over time, I began to see that what once isolated me could also empower me. My lived experience gave me a perspective that others did not have, a lens through which I could notice gaps, question assumptions, and spark new ideas.

I had spent so much of my life believing that I was unworthy, that I was not enough. I will never forget the first time my husband told me I was beautiful. My instinctive reaction was not gratitude or joy, it was disbelief. I genuinely thought he was mocking me. I had been conditioned to see myself through the lens of rejection, to the point where I couldn't even recognise sincerity when it was offered to me.

Over time, I also started to see how my different perspective could add value.

In the Arctic, self-awareness was not optional. Every small decision mattered, how much I drank, how I layered my clothing, even how I carried my sled. One day, I ignored the early signs of frostnip on my fingers because I did not want to be seen as slowing the group down. I told myself it was nothing. But that choice left a lasting impact. Even now, when the weather turns cold, I still feel a sharp reminder in my fingertips.

That moment taught me something lasting - self-awareness is not just about emotions or personality. it is about paying attention to your needs whether physical, emotional, or mental, before they become problems.

In the workplace, I have seen the same pattern: leaders who push through burnout, who silence doubts, who ignore discomfort, until something breaks. Self-awareness gives us the early signals. But only if we're willing to listen.

In meetings, I would suggest ideas that seemed obvious to me, but others would react as if I had just uncovered something revolutionary. It was not that I was any smarter; it was simply that my lived experience had given me a different lens through which to see the world. I had learned to spot gaps where others saw a complete picture, to notice details that others overlooked. And slowly, I began to realise that what made me different also made me valuable.

The very things that made me feel isolated as a child became the foundation of who I am today.

I learned resilience not from bravery, but from the need to survive; by getting back up every time I was knocked down.

I learned empathy because I knew, deep in my bones, what it felt like to be left out, and I promised myself I would never let others feel that same invisible sting.

And I learned courage by refusing to let the world define my worth. Even when I doubted myself, even when I felt I did not belong, I kept showing up. I chose to persist, even when it would have been easier to disappear.

Broadening how we see diversity

For too long, diversity has been reduced to something we can see, usually race or gender. But true diversity runs much deeper than appearances. It lives in our minds, our histories, our ways of thinking, and the quiet, often overlooked stories we carry.

It lives in the colleague managing a chronic health condition that is not visible to the eye. In the autistic team member who sees patterns others miss. In the carer who balances spreadsheets by day and their parent's medication by night. In the single mother returning to work after years of raising children, uncertain whether she still belongs. In the refugee who brings global insight, shaped by resilience most of us can only imagine.

It is in the deep thinker who doesn't speak unless they've really thought something through. The person who skips after-work drinks, not because they're antisocial, but because that space was never designed with them in mind. It is in the veteran adjusting to civilian life after years of military service. In the introvert who notices what no one else does in a noisy meeting room.

Diversity is not just difference you can name. It is also difference you might miss, unless you're looking closely, listening fully, and creating space for others to show up as they are.

When we define diversity too narrowly, we end up silencing the very people who could enrich our teams the most. Because those who do not fit our limited view of what difference 'looks like' are often left out of the conversation.

True inclusion asks us to widen the lens. To move beyond categories. To start seeing people not only for what they represent, but for the unique richness they bring.

Why diversity matters

Diversity is not just about representation. It is not about hiring people who look different to fill a quota. It is about recognising, valuing, and leveraging differences to build stronger, more innovative, and more inclusive communities.

We often discuss diversity as though it is a checkbox, something to achieve. But diversity is not a goal, it isa reality. The real question is: *How do we choose to engage with it?*

When we embrace diversity, we challenge our own assumptions. We expand our perspectives. We create spaces where more people feel seen, heard, and valued.

And most importantly, we remind each other that being different is not something to fix, it is something to celebrate!

For so many years, I wished I could hide my differences. Today, I stand in rooms where those differences are my greatest asset. That little girl who once wished she could change, now understands the truth: belonging is not about being the same, it is about being accepted as you are. And that is the kind of world I want to help build.

BEYOND THE ICE

From isolation to strength - Finding belonging in the harshest conditions:

For most of my life, I fought to prove that I belonged. I believed that blending in would earn me acceptance. But belonging is not about suppressing who you are; it is about being valued for what you bring. And I did not fully realise that until I found myself in the Arctic, where thriving depended on recognising our differences rather than hiding them.

In the Arctic, there were no mirrors, no reminders of what set me apart. The only thing that mattered was overcoming adversity, and that was only possible through trust, collaboration, and embracing each person's strengths, no matter how different they were.

At first, the old instincts kicked in. I questioned whether I was strong enough, capable enough, or if I would once again be the outsider. Would I be the weak link? Would my teammates see me as different? But the Arctic had no patience for self-doubt. Out there, my value was not based on how I looked or whether I fit in; it was based on what I could contribute. And that changed everything-

The Arctic - Where differences became strengths

At first glance, our Arctic expedition appeared to be a team of equals: twelve women, each determined and physically and mentally prepared for the challenge ahead. But beneath the surface, we were all vastly different. Different backgrounds, different skill sets, different life experiences. In most workplaces, these differences might have been seen as obstacles, potential sources of friction. But in the Arctic, they were what kept us alive.

Diverse strengths in action

In the Arctic, past job roles and achievements faded into the background. What mattered most was how we showed up for one another, moment by moment.

We each had our strengths

Some of us were natural problem-solvers. When our sleds tipped over in the deep snow, it was the engineers and the meticulous planners who instinctively implemented better weight distribution.

Some were physically strong. They took turns breaking the trail through fresh snow, pushing forward when the rest of us needed a moment to recover.

Some were intuitive leaders. They sensed when someone was struggling - whether physically or emotionally - and stepped in with a word of encouragement or a helping hand.

And then there were unexpected moments, times when we surprised ourselves. The quietest among us turned out to be the most perceptive, noticing small signs of fatigue or frostbite before they became real dangers. Others who weren't the fastest skiers proved invaluable in setting up camp efficiently, ensuring we had shelter before the temperatures dropped even further.

The moment I understood the power of differences

One evening, after an exhausting day of pulling sleds in punishing cold, tensions flared. The cold was suffocating, and exhaustion made even the smallest tasks feel impossible. Someone suggested a new way to distribute the workload, rotating responsibilities to ensure no one was stuck doing the most gruelling jobs every night.

At first, there was resistance. People had their own ways of doing things, their own routines. But we tried it. And it worked. It was a simple shift, but it proved something more significant; we weren't just surviving individually, we were adapting together. We were stronger because of our differences, not in spite of them.

Lesson: True diversity goes beyond visible differences. It is about the value we place on diverse lived experiences, perspectives, and ways of thinking. Whether in the Arctic or in the boardroom, it is our differences that strengthen resilience, deepen connection, and spark innovation. When we stop trying to blend in and instead show up fully as ourselves, we unlock the true power of inclusion, for individuals and for the collective.

Understanding diversity, inclusion, and belonging

These three words - diversity, inclusion, and belonging - are often grouped together as if they mean the same thing. But they don't. Each one asks something different of us. And when we do not take the time to understand them clearly, we risk missing the deeper work each one invites.

I remember delivering a workshop at a remote site in the UK. Everyone in the room was white, and when we began exploring why there was not more visible diversity in the organisation, someone said, "Well, there's nobody like that around here." They weren't being defensive; it was just their reality. For them, diversity was about who lived nearby. If they did not see people of colour, people with a disability, or someone with a different social background around them, then diversity was not seen as relevant.

But that moment echoed in my mind. Because it reflected something deeper: how we often think of diversity as a numbers game - who's present, who's visible - rather than as a question of access, outreach, or even intention. Diversity is not about ticking boxes. it is about asking: *Who's missing, and why?* And what are we doing (or not doing) that might be contributing to that absence?

Diversity is the first layer. It is about who is in the room. Who's at the table? Who gets through the door in the first place? And sometimes, understanding that the door is not even visible to those who've never had to knock.

Inclusion is something else entirely. It is about what happens once you're in. Do you get to speak? Are your ideas listened to? Are you constantly interrupted, overlooked, or expected to assimilate? Inclusion is about making sure everyone can participate fully, not just be present.

And then there's belonging. That is the most personal of all. Belonging is not about being invited, it is about no longer feeling the need to ask. It is the quiet confidence that says, *"I can be myself here, and I am still respected."*

These aren't just corporate buzzwords. They're steps. First, we recognise who's missing (diversity). Then, we create spaces where everyone can participate meaningfully (inclusion). And only then can we build environments where people feel safe enough to be themselves (belonging).

Mini reflection on privilege

Privilege doesn't mean your life has been easy. It means there are certain challenges you haven't had to face simply because of aspects of your identity.

It might be walking into a room and seeing yourself reflected in the leadership team. Or going through life without having to explain your name, your accent, or your body. Or being assumed competent before you've even said a word.

I have walked into rooms where I have been mistaken for the cleaner or asked to fetch the coffee when I was the speaker. That is the absence of privilege, and it chips away at your confidence over time.

These moments are rarely about intent. But they quietly remind us who is expected to lead, and who is not. This is what a lack of privilege can look like.

Recognising privilege is not about guilt. It is about awareness. Once we see the unearned advantages some of us have, we can start using them to lift others up.

The invisible barrier - Understanding the glass ceiling

Some people walk into a workplace already seen as leadership material. Others hit a ceiling they can't see but can feel. That is the glass ceiling.

It is the unspoken limit placed on the progression of women, people of colour, disabled professionals, or anyone whose identity doesn't match what traditional leadership has looked like. It is not always overt. No one says, "You can't lead." Instead, opportunities quietly pass by. High-visibility projects go to someone else. Promotions stall without explanation. Feedback becomes vague. The rules shift, but only for some.

I have worked with incredibly talented individuals who were told they weren't quite 'ready' for promotion, despite years of strong performance. Yet others, with fewer results, were labelled 'potential' simply because they fit the image of leadership that people were used to.

The glass ceiling is not always a single moment of rejection. Often, it is a pattern. A series of small exclusions, slow delays, or decisions made in rooms you were never invited into.

But here's another layer we do not talk about enough. Even those who have traditionally benefited from privilege can reach a point where the system no longer serves them either. I have met white leaders who, after climbing the corporate ladder, suddenly found themselves stuck. Not because of bias, but because the structure was too narrow, built for hierarchy, not growth.

When leadership space is limited, everyone eventually bumps into the ceiling. And in systems that reward sameness, innovation slows for everyone.

So this is not just about making room for underrepresented voices. It is about creating better systems, for all of us. Because when leadership becomes more inclusive, more flexible, more open, everyone gets to grow.

Moving beyond tokenism - Creating real inclusion

Diversity is not about optics. It is about opportunity. Hiring underrepresented talent without giving them a voice, influence, or real agency is not inclusion. It is tokenism.

Tokenism says, *"You can be here, but only on our terms."* True inclusion says, *"We want your voice at the table, and we're willing to change because of what we hear."*

The problem with tokenism is that it often coexists with privilege. Those with privilege may not see the barriers others face. They may assume inclusion has been achieved just because someone is 'in the room.' But being present is not the same as being empowered.

When people feel like they've been invited to check a box, not to contribute meaningfully, they disengage, or they leave.

True inclusion is about the redistribution of influence, not just representation. It means changing who gets to ask the questions, who sets the agenda, and who makes the decisions.

Lessons from the Arctic - Why diversity matters in every environment

If we had all been the same, if we had all approached problems in the same way, we wouldn't have made it. It was our differences that allowed us to push through.

Diversity of thought - Different decision-making styles

Some of us were analytical, preferring to assess risks carefully before taking action. Others relied on instinct, trusting their gut to guide us. When we got caught in a whiteout, this mix of perspectives was invaluable. Some wanted to wait it out and assess the risks, while others wanted to push forward before conditions worsened, and some suggested rerouting.

Our final decision was not one extreme. It was a combination of all three approaches, ensuring we continued to move forward without unnecessary risk.

Diversity of skills - Problem solving in crisis

One day, as we pushed forward through the icy terrain, we hit a hidden boulder beneath the snow. The impact sent a jolt through one of the sleds, cracking part of its frame and shifting the load. By the time we stopped to assess the damage, we realised that some of our supplies had gotten wet, an enormous challenge in those temperatures. Wet gear meant colder nights, and colder nights meant less rest and increased risk.

While most of us worried about how we would manage, one of our guides, experienced in extreme conditions, stepped in without hesitation. Using rope and an ice axe, they reinforced the frame - an imperfect fix - but enough to keep us moving.

That night, as one of the team struggled to dry out their gear and get warm, I realised that problem-solving is not always about having the perfect solution; it is about making the best decision with what you have.

Diversity of experience - Different ways of coping

Exhaustion tested us all, but we each handled it in our own way. Some needed silence to stay focused. Some cracked jokes to break the tension. A few relied on small rituals, like double-checking gear before setting off, to maintain a sense of control. There was no right way to cope, but understanding each other's needs made us a stronger team.

BEYOND THE ICE

The Arctic lesson - From endurance to innovation

In the workplace, we frequently discussed diversity. However, it is often treated as a compliance requirement rather than a strategic advantage.

In the Arctic, our well-being depended on diversity, not just in identity but in thought, skills, and problem-solving. The same is true in the workplace. True innovation comes when we harness diverse strengths, not just tolerate them.

Just as our differences in skills, strengths, and perspectives helped us survive in the Arctic, they also drive innovation, collaboration, and long-term success in organisations.

Whether in extreme environments or corporate boardrooms, it is never about individual strength. It is about collective resilience.

From the Arctic to the boardroom - Why diversity matters everywhere

Out in the Arctic, our differences were not obstacles. They were assets. Each of us brought something unique to the team, and in an environment where success depended on collaboration, those differences became our greatest strength.

But what about in the workplace?

Too often, differences are overlooked or even seen as barriers rather than strategic advantages. Yet the same lessons from the Arctic, valuing diverse perspectives, leveraging unique strengths, and working together toward a shared goal, are just as critical in the workplace.

Some organisations have recognised this and turned diversity into a competitive advantage.

A company that transformed inclusion into success

One company I worked with, a large financial services firm, was struggling to integrate diverse perspectives into leadership decision-making. They prided themselves on hiring from a wide range of backgrounds, yet a small, homogeneous group still dominated senior leadership decisions.

The result was a slow erosion of trust and engagement. Talented employees were leaving, not because they lacked ability, but because they did not feel heard or valued. Innovation had started to plateau, with the same voices presenting the same solutions. Even their clients, whose needs and expectations were rapidly evolving, were beginning to sense the disconnect.

When I first met with their executive team, they were aware of the problem but did not fully grasp the cost of not addressing it. Leadership expressed their commitment to diversity, yet their boardroom still resembled the one it had ten years ago.

"I posed a question that shifted the room, *"Who is missing from the conversation?"*

A silence filled the room. Glances were exchanged. The realisation sank in.

They had built a pipeline of diverse talent, but they hadn't opened the gate. Only a fraction of their workforce was shaping the company's future.

What we did differently

Rather than deliver another generic diversity workshop, we focused on embedding inclusive leadership into the very fabric of decision-making. We worked across three key areas.

First, we looked at how diverse talent could be better activated. Leaders were coached to actively involve underrepresented team members in strategic discussions, ensuring that new and different voices were contributing where it mattered most.

Second, we introduced a reverse mentoring programme, where traditional roles are flipped, and senior leaders are mentored by employees from underrepresented groups. We paired individuals from diverse backgrounds with senior executives, giving leaders direct, personal insight into what it felt like to navigate the organisation from a different vantage point. These relationships helped reveal barriers that traditional reporting had missed.

Third, we established inclusive innovation panels. Before any major strategy was signed off, leaders were asked to consult with employees from a cross-section of the business. These conversations provided insight that was fresh, relevant, and often game-changing.

The Results

Within 18 months, the leadership landscape began to change. Thirty percent of new senior appointments came from underrepresented backgrounds, a significant shift in an industry where diversity was typically slow to progress.

Innovation surged, with employee-led initiatives increasing by 46 percent. The energy was different. New ideas were flowing, client engagement strategies evolved, and people across the business began to feel seen and heard.

Retention also improved, with turnover among diverse talent dropping by 27 percent. Employees weren't just staying because of the salary or the brand. They were staying because they felt valued.

These changes weren't driven by ticking boxes. They came from intention. Leaders changed how they showed up. They listened differently. They acted.

And the organisation grew stronger because of it.

When we change the way we lead, we change the way we succeed.

When inclusion is more than a headline

Diversity is not about appearances. It is about meaningful action. Hiring underrepresented talent without giving them influence or agency is not inclusion. It is tokenism.

When people sense that they have been included just to meet a quota rather than for their genuine contributions, they often disengage. True inclusion is not about having a seat at the table for show. It is about ensuring that diverse perspectives are listened to, respected, and acted upon.

While some organisations continue to struggle with tokenism, others have embedded inclusion into their culture, values, and decision-making. The results speak for themselves.

Proving it works at scale - Johnson & Johnson

Johnson & Johnson is one example of a company where inclusion is not a side project but an integral part of how they do business.

Johnson & Johnson is one organisation that has built diversity and inclusion into the core of its business model. Rather than treating diversity as a compliance issue, they actively link it to innovation and growth.

Their executive leaders are held accountable through tangible measures, including diversity-related performance indicators that influence their bonuses. This ensures that inclusion is not just a promise but a priority.

By applying inclusive design thinking, they involve a wide range of voices in product development. This means their healthcare solutions are shaped by the people who will actually use them, leading to better, more inclusive outcomes.

The impact is measurable. Research by McKinsey & Company shows that companies with higher levels of racial and ethnic diversity are 35 percent more likely to financially outperform their industry peers.

Diverse teams do more than enhance an organisation's image. They unlock creativity, drive stronger business results, and create cultures that are more responsive and resilient.

But for diversity to be truly meaningful, we must move beyond hiring people who look different. We must make space for them to lead, to influence, and to shape what comes next.

Why diversity must move from theory to practice

Whether we are enduring adversity in the harshest conditions or tackling challenges in the workplace, success rarely comes from sameness. It comes from recognising and drawing strength from our differences.

The companies that will thrive are not those that treat diversity as a box to tick. They are the ones that embed inclusion into how they lead, how they innovate, and how they grow.

True diversity is not just about hiring people who look different. It is about ensuring that everyone has a seat at the table and a voice that is genuinely heard.

Bias is not always visible in policies. More often, it hides in the quiet, everyday moments that shape culture, the offhand comments, the decisions made without input, the assumptions left unchallenged.

Inclusion is not a checkbox or a single training session. It is the foundation of resilience, innovation, and long-term success.

When we treat difference as strength and not as something to work around, we change the way we lead and the way we live. That shift begins not with sweeping statements but with everyday choices, to see, to hear, and to include.

Reflection Prompt

Think back to a time when you felt different, because of your identity, background, or beliefs.

What helped you feel seen and valued in that moment?

Now consider: who in your world today might still be waiting to feel that sense of belonging?

Call to Action

Diversity is not something to manage. It is something to honour.

In your workplace, pause and ask: whose perspectives are missing from key conversations?

In your personal life, explore stories and experiences different from your own.

In any space you occupy, be the person who sees others, includes others, and invites difference as a strength.

These are not grand gestures. They are everyday choices that build inclusive, human-centred communities.

Final Thought

For much of my life, I believed that belonging meant fitting in. That I had to mute parts of myself just to be accepted.

BEYOND THE ICE

But over time, I have learned that what sets us apart is often where our greatest power lies.

True diversity is not about ticking boxes. It is about seeing difference as essential.

It is about listening deeply. Acting intentionally. And leading with care.

When we honour difference, we do more than build better teams.

We build a better future, one where everyone gets to thrive.

Notes

CHAPTER 10
Belonging - The journey back to myself

"To be yourself in a world that is constantly trying to make you something else is the greatest accomplishment."- Ralph Waldo Emerson

We often think of belonging as something we reach once others accept us. But what if it is not about arrival at all? What if it is about remembering who we've always been? A quiet, rooted feeling inside us: the kind that whispers, *you are enough, just as you are.*

For much of my life, I searched for that feeling. I looked for it in classrooms where I was the only brown girl, in workplaces where I was the only one with my accent, and even in a family photo where I did not resemble anyone. I did not have the language for it back then, but I felt the quiet ache of not recognising myself (or being recognised) in any space I entered.

I learned early on that fitting in often meant hiding parts of myself to match the space around me. Fitting in is about contorting yourself to match the space around you. I remember being at school and trying to mimic how the other girls spoke, styled their hair, or carried themselves, hoping that if I mirrored them closely enough, I might blend in. I laughed when I did not feel like it, stayed silent when something felt wrong, and avoided speaking about where I was really from. It was not belonging. It was performance. And over time, I started losing sight of who I actually was. Belonging is about taking up space without apology. It is not about being tolerated, it is about being valued, for exactly who you are.

In this chapter, we will explore the quiet but powerful shift from fitting in, to truly belonging. We will reflect on what it means to stop seeking permission and begin accepting ourselves as we are. You will travel with me back to India, where my journey began, and into the Arctic, where I finally saw my own reflection more clearly. Through stories from childhood, the workplace, and extreme environments, we will see that belonging is not granted – it is created. And we will discover that before we can help others feel included, we must learn to accept ourselves, as we are.

A journey back to where it all began

In 2019, I boarded a plane to India, a place that had existed only in stories, in photographs, and in the corners of my mind. It was my birthplace, but not a place with which I was familiar. I had no memories of my time there, no emotional ties. And yet, as the plane touched down, I felt something unexpected: a quiet pull, as if I were returning to a part of myself, I had never truly known.

For most of my life, India was a word on a birth certificate. A birthplace I could name but not remember. It rarely entered my day-to-day thoughts, tucked away like a closed chapter I had never opened. Then one evening, I watched the film *Lion*. If you've seen it, you will know, it is the story of a young Indian boy, adopted by an Australian family, who finds his way back to his birth mother decades later. That film stirred something I hadn't known was still there; a quiet, persistent longing to understand where I come from and what I had left behind

That film became a catalyst. For the first time, I let myself ask the questions I had avoided for years. Who was I before I was adopted? What parts of my story had been left behind? What might my life have looked like if I had stayed in India?

I was not chasing closure or expecting life-changing revelations. But I knew I needed to see it with my own eyes. To walk the streets where my story began. To connect with a version of myself I had never fully acknowledged.

Finding the place I once belonged

Through faded documents and worn photographs, I began piecing together the fragments of a story I had never dared to explore. Each discovery felt like a breadcrumb leading me back to the beginning. Eventually, my search took me to a small orphanage in Bangalore, the very place where I had spent the first two years of my life.

And it was there that I found her. Sister Regina.

She had cared for me as a baby, and although decades had passed, she remembered me. Not just my name or my file, but *me*. Her face lit up with recognition, and in that moment, something inside me settled. It felt like someone had been holding a thread from my past all along.

I visited the hospital where they still worked, where so many babies, just like me, had been left in baskets, wrapped in blankets, waiting for a chance at life. I walked through the children's quarters, saw where they ate, where they learned, where they slept. And for the first time, I could imagine it. A version of my life that might have been.

What if I had grown up here? What if I had never left India? Would I have known this building not as a visitor, but as home? Would I have worn a school uniform, spoken fluent Kannada, played in this very courtyard?

I was not there for answers. I was there for truth. And the truth I found was quiet but powerful. I was not returning as a child in need. I was returning as a woman carrying her own story.

The moment everything came full circle

While I was there, I was invited to deliver a keynote speech to a group of young women training to become doctors. These women had grown up in orphanages, just like I had. Their beginnings were marked by struggle, uncertainty, and systems that too often overlook potential.

They were on a path of incredible purpose, choosing to dedicate their lives to healing others. And there I stood before them - not with a medical degree or a long list of accolades - but with my story.

I did not arrive with answers, only with honesty. I spoke of the doubts I had carried, the longing to belong, and the journey I had taken to find strength in my identity. As I shared, I saw something in their eyes, a quiet admiration, yes, but also a deep recognition. They saw in me a future that was possible. And I saw in them the same courage I had once searched for in myself.

That day, something shifted. The same little girl who once stood in front of a mirror wishing to be someone else was now standing in a room full of young women, each rewriting their own future. I no longer needed to rewrite who I was. In their eyes, I saw the reflection I had long searched for in myself. And for the first time, I felt proud of every part of my story. Together, we proved that where we begin does not limit where we can go.

For most of my life, I had believed that my birth mother had died. It was the story I had been told and the one I carried quietly for decades. But in 2019, a friend helped me uncover something I never expected. Through a private investigation, we discovered that no official death certificate had ever been found. Alongside that came my original birth certificate, a document I had never seen, but one that revealed a different birth date from the one I had always known. As I held it in my hands, it felt as if the ground had shifted beneath me. I spent months processing what it meant to have such a vital part of my identity rewritten in an instant. In India, it is not uncommon for records to be misplaced, facts to be lost, or never recorded at all. But what mattered now was that this discovery opened the door to a new possibility. My birth mother might still be out there. And perhaps the story I had accepted all these years was not the whole truth.

That revelation did not just shake my past. It led me to take the first step toward finding the truth for myself.

The return to my roots - Lessons from the nuns in India

When I returned to India, I expected to find pieces of the past, fragments of a life I had never truly known. I thought I would uncover facts, maybe names, perhaps some history. But instead, I was met with something far more profound: unconditional welcome.

The nuns who had once cared for me as a baby opened their arms and their hearts, without hesitation. There was no awkwardness, no formality. Only warmth. Only presence. There were no questions to answer, no credentials to prove. No expectation that I explain who I had become. Just a quiet but unshakable acceptance.

In that moment, I was not a stranger returning to a place I barely remembered; I was someone who had never truly left their hearts. That moment changed me.

It reminded me that belonging is not something we earn. It is not conditional. It is not transactional. It is something we can offer each other, freely and without reservation.

These women didn't just run an orphanage. They created something sacred: a home. A home that was never really lost. A place where every child, regardless of their story or how many years had passed, was still seen as one of their own.

It didn't matter how long I'd been gone. It didn't matter how far life had taken me. To them, I was still their child.

And that moment, quiet and grounding, taught me something I carry with me even now; belonging is never out of reach. The door is never truly closed. Sometimes, it has been open all along, waiting for us to step through.

Still searching - A piece of the story not yet complete

Even though I found so many pieces of my story when I returned to India, there is still one part I haven't been able to follow. I have not yet found my birth mother. I even took a DNA test, hoping it might offer some answers, but still, the connection remains elusive. I have travelled across continents, retraced forgotten paths, and stood on the soil where my life began.

I have not met her, and yet I feel her presence in quiet, persistent ways; in my skin, in my questions, in the echo of something I still cannot name. There are days when the longing feels sharp, like something just out of reach. I imagine the feel of her hug, the sound of her voice. I dream of owning even a single photo I could treasure for the rest of my life. Some circles are not yet closed. But that doesn't mean the story is unfinished.

This search is not about rejecting or disrespecting my adoptive family. It is not rooted in anger or resentment. It is about understanding, about tracing the shape of a history I never got to know. It is about seeing the roots of a family tree I have always carried but never seen.

BEYOND THE ICE

I am incredibly grateful for the love and care my adoptive family has given me. They took me in with open hearts, and I will always carry that gratitude. But this journey is not about diminishing that love or feeling like I owe them anything. It is simply about wanting to know the truth of my origins. I have been raised with love, but the story of my beginning remains incomplete.

When you adopt a child, you do so with your heart. You take them into your family not because of obligation, but because of love and compassion. That act of love is what makes a family, regardless of biological ties. I believe that when you adopt, you give a child the gift of not just a home, but a place to truly belong. No matter the outcome, the love you offer is enough.

Part of my own journey has been rooted in the importance of understanding where I come from. This is why I wanted to bring my children to India, to help them discover their own roots. We spent time here as a family, visiting the magnificent Taj Mahal and experiencing a land filled with history and connection. In doing so, I wanted them to feel the power of understanding their heritage, and how it can shape who we are today.

I am not trying to rewrite the past. I am simply trying to make sense of it. If I could meet my birth mother, I wouldn't ask why. I would thank her. Thank her for giving me life. For letting me go. For making a decision that must have broken her heart and yet made mine possible. That one act, full of pain and courage, led me to my husband, to my children, and to a life filled with meaning. Yes, the beginning of my life did not follow the storybook script. But when I look at everything that has grown from that early sacrifice, I do not see loss. I see legacy. I see love. I see purpose.

Not every circle closes the way we imagine. Sometimes, closure is not the gift. The gift is the path itself. Belonging doesn't always come from answers. Sometimes, it comes from continuing the journey with grace, with hope, and with an open heart. And until I find her, or even if I never do, I will keep walking. I will keep searching. And I will keep honouring the story that brought me here. Whether it was the orphanage in Bangalore or the frozen silence of the Arctic, each place helped me return to a part of myself I had long forgotten.

Lesson: Belonging is not something we earn

I used to think that being included meant I had to fit in first. But real belonging begins when you stop seeking external approval and start accepting yourself. It is not about proving your worth to others. It is about believing you were already enough.

Belonging is not a prize for good behaviour or perfect assimilation. It is the quiet power of knowing who you are and choosing to stand in that truth, even if no one else offers you a seat.

When we create space for others to belong, we affirm that they do not need to change in order to be included. And when we claim that same space for ourselves, we lead by example.

I spent much of my life chasing a sense of belonging. I tried to be what others expected, shaping myself to feel worthy, to feel seen. But the journey back to my birthplace, to that small orphanage in Bangalore, revealed something I hadn't understood before.

I was not searching for a home. I *was* the home.

Belonging was not something I had to earn. It was something I had to remember.

And maybe that is the truth for all of us.

We do not find belonging in other people's approval. We find it when we stop hiding, when we return to ourselves, and when we finally say, "I am enough."

BEYOND THE ICE

The Arctic - Finding strength in my own reflection

Belonging beyond expectations

More than a hundred women applied to join the Arctic expedition. Only twelve were selected. Each of us came with our own reasons, our own personal mountains to climb. But underneath it all, we were looking for more than adventure. We were searching for something deeper - belonging.

For so much of our lives, we had played roles dictated by society: as mothers, daughters, wives, caregivers, employees. We had been told what we could and couldn't do, how far we could go, what we should aspire to. But deep inside, each of us wanted to push past those limitations. We wanted to prove, to ourselves more than anyone else, that we were capable of more. That we had a place not just in our homes, our jobs, or our families, but in the vastness of the world itself.

In the Arctic, we saw how even those who didn't cross the ice still shaped the journey. I explore that in more depth in the next chapter – because their story is a powerful lesson in true belonging.

Belonging is not only about the people who make it to the finish line; it is about the entire journey, and everyone who walks beside you, even when their path takes a different turn.

As you know by now, as part of the expedition, our company had selected twelve women to ski 100 kilometres across Baffin Island, in what turned out to be -43°C conditions, the harshest Arctic Spring the local Innuits had seen in years.

But ours was not the only story.

Alongside us, three incredible women were chosen as reserves.
They trained with us, dragging car tyres across muddy parks at dawn and dusk, whether it was raining, hailing, or snowing, replicating the sled-pulling we would later face on the ice. And they did it all knowing there was a very big chance they might never go. That they might prepare with full dedication for something they wouldn't fully experience.

If that is not commitment, what is?

They weren't just "on standby." They were part of us. They shared the same preparation, the same anticipation, just without the certainty.

One of them told me recently, "I had already made peace with the fact I was not going." That was her way of protecting herself. Because how do you stay committed to something that may never happen and you have no control over?

That kind of emotional strength, to stay present, to show up anyway, is a courage of its own.

Then, just ten days before departure, the unthinkable happened…
Our expedition leader, the woman who had spent four years planning and building this project, broke her leg in a skiing accident. Her dream and her vision,

collapsed in a moment. And with it came a space no one had expected.

The reserves received a message: one of them would be called up. The decision would be made within hours.

Two of them, working side by side in the same room on the same project, waited in silence for the phone to ring.

Can you imagine that moment? The hope. The heartbreak. The guilt of wanting something that might come at your friend's expense.

One of them got the call.

She stepped into the team with quiet determination, carrying not only her own excitement, but also the weight of the woman who couldn't come. I often think about what that must have felt like, to join a bonded group so close to departure, to carry that duality of gratitude and grief.

It takes bravery to go. But it also takes bravery to stay.

What about the two reserves who remained?

Their story matters just as much. It is easy to celebrate the ones who cross the ice. But the ones who train just as hard, who carry their own complex emotions, who support from the sidelines without recognition, they are part of this legacy too.

As we left for the airport, unbeknown to us, our HR director made a call. The two remaining reserves would be flown out to meet us at the finish line. And they did. They skied a short distance, met the Innuits, and reunited with us, along with our injured expedition leader and Sally, my original tent buddy, who had twisted her ankle mid-way through the journey.

Their arrival marked something profound; a circle closed, a team made whole again.

Their story was different. But it was no less meaningful.

Because every tent told a different story. Every woman lived her own version of the expedition. And every contribution, whether made on the ice, in the months of training, or at the final reunion, shaped this experience.

That is the truth about belonging. It doesn't come from a shared outcome. It comes from shared purpose. From walking beside each other, even when the destination is uncertain.

Comfort zones are cosy, but nothing life-changing happens there

None of us had ever skied across an Arctic landscape, never faced temperatures as brutal as -40°C. This was not comfortable. This was not easy. But that was the point.

Stepping outside our comfort zones was never just about the cold. It was about shedding the quiet narratives we had been handed our whole lives. The ones that said *"You do not belong here. This is not for you."*

For years, we had been conditioned to believe that extreme environments, endurance challenges, and feats of self-preservation were reserved for someone else. Someone stronger. Someone more experienced. Someone who looked different to us. But the moment we stepped onto the ice, we *became* those people.

Growth, transformation, and self-discovery do not happen in safety. They happen in the unknown, in the struggle, in the willingness to say, "I am more than what I have been told." Because if your goals do not scare you, they're not stretching you enough.

The Arctic was never just about the cold

When we set foot on that glacial stretch, we didn't just step into the unknown, we stepped into a version of ourselves that had always been waiting to emerge. There were no titles or labels out there. It didn't matter whether someone was a CEO, a stay-at-home mother, or a student. It didn't matter what our race, background, or life experience was. The only thing that mattered was how we showed up for ourselves and for each other.

The doubts were loud. The cold seeped into every bone. The sleds were heavy, and exhaustion weighed on both body and mind. There were moments when I wondered if I had made a mistake, if I had truly earned my place. But then I looked around me. I was not alone.

Every time I stumbled, someone offered a hand. Every time the wind howled through our tents, someone whispered words of encouragement. When the ice cracked beneath our feet, we moved together, united by purpose and trust.

The Arctic taught me something that years of searching had not: belonging is not something you earn. It is something you create.

We did not belong because we had passed a test. We belonged because we showed up with our full selves. Because we chose to believe we were enough.

Lesson: Belonging is a choice, not a prize

For so long, I had believed that belonging had to be granted by others. That someone had to see me, to say the words, "You belong here," before I could believe it for myself. But the Arctic showed me something very different.

Stop waiting for permission - If you've ever held back because you did not feel "ready enough", ask yourself this: *Who are you waiting for? What would it look like to back yourself without needing approval?*

Challenge the idea that you do not belong - Think of a space where you've doubted your place. What would change if you walked into it with the belief that you deserve to be there?

Do one thing this week that stretches you - Speak up. Sign up. Show up. You do not need to be fearless, just willing.

Make belonging a daily action - Who around you might be doubting their place? A quiet word, a genuine invitation, a moment of recognition can shift everything.

Take up space with quiet confidence - Not by proving your worth, but by knowing it. You belong because you are here. And that is enough.

A place to thrive - From extreme environments to everyday leadership

The Arctic was never just about resilience. It was about discovering that the place we'd been searching for has always lived within us.

I travelled across the globe, dragged a heavy sled across frozen ground, and endured bitter cold, all in the hope of finding something I thought I lacked. But what I discovered out there was not something new. It was a truth I had forgotten; I belonged not because someone said so, but because I finally believed it myself.

And I hope you know this too. Belonging is not earned. It is remembered.

For years, organisations have talked about diversity and inclusion. But true belonging goes further. It is not just about hiring diverse teams, it is about creating an environment where people feel valued, respected, and safe to be themselves.

Too often, companies treat diversity as a goal – a quota to meet, or a box to tick. But diversity without inclusion is merely optics. And diversity without belonging is a missed opportunity.

True belonging means creating space where people are not expected to edit who they are just to be accepted. Where they can bring their ideas, identity, and experiences to the table without fear of judgement or exclusion.

BEYOND THE ICE

I have walked into boardrooms as the only person of colour. The only woman. The only one with my accent or background. I have felt the silent question in the room – *why are you here?*

I have also felt the transformation when that question is replaced with a different one: *"What do you think? What do you see that we might not?"*

That is what belonging looks like – not just being present, but being heard, trusted, and empowered to lead.

Belonging in the workplace is not about blending in. It is about feeling safe enough to stand out. I have seen this at Microsoft, where inclusive design begins with empathy and leads to innovation. They embedded empathy into leadership and empowered employee voices to shape policy. That shift didn't just change culture. It transformed performance.

I have seen what it looks like when someone walks into a meeting and chooses to stay silent, not because they have nothing to say, but because they're unsure if their voice matters. I have met people who hide parts of who they are, the accent they tone down, the hobbies they do not mention, the photos they remove from their desks, all in the hope of avoiding judgment have seen people invited into the room but never truly welcomed into the conversation. They are present, but their voices are ignored. It sends a quiet message: you are here to observe, not to contribute

But then, I have also seen what belonging really looks like.

It is the leader who turns and says, "What do you think?" and then actually listens to the reply. It is the moment someone shares an idea and it is not only acknowledged, but built upon. It is the feeling of being seen, not as an outsider or a risk, but as an essential part of the conversation.

Belonging creates the space for people to thrive. It transforms a room from a place of performance into a place of possibility. When people feel valued for who they are, not *despite* their differences, but *because* of them, they do not just stay. They soar.

Above & Beyond Resilience - A case study in cultural change

Due to confidentiality agreements, the client's name cannot be disclosed. However, this case study reflects real-world impact and demonstrates how inclusive leadership can drive meaningful change.

This organisation had strong hiring policies and diversity training in place. On paper, they were doing everything right. But people from underrepresented backgrounds were still leaving. Why? Because they did not feel they belonged.

I was brought in to support the leadership team. Instead of launching another generic training module, we began with honest conversations. We explored key questions:

- What signals are you unconsciously sending to your teams?
- Who is always heard? Who is routinely overlooked?
- Are you mentoring, or are you advocating? Are you opening doors?

We moved from policy to practice.

Through a series of coaching sessions, reflective exercises, and 360-degree feedback, we helped leaders move from well-meaning intent to measurable change. One senior leader, during a facilitated discussion, heard a colleague share how overlooked she felt when her ideas were routinely dismissed in meetings. It struck him that he had never noticed this pattern, not because he disagreed, but because it had never happened to him. That moment became a turning point. Rather than becoming defensive, he acknowledged his blind spot in front of his team. He committed to change, not through grand speeches, but by adjusting daily behaviours: inviting quieter voices into discussions, pausing to ask who hadn't spoken, and setting a new norm where every perspective was expected, not optional. He also asked his direct reports to hold him accountable by giving real-time feedback in meetings.

Within six months:

- Engagement scores rose by 24%.
- Retention improved by 18%.
- Diverse leadership pipeline increased by 36%.

This didn't happen through radical restructuring. It happened because leaders started leading with intention. Because they made belonging part of their daily behaviour, not just their strategy slides.

Inclusive leadership in action - The Microsoft example

When Satya Nadella stepped into his role as CEO of Microsoft in 2014, he did not begin by reshaping the company's performance targets. He began by reshaping its culture.

He introduced empathy as a leadership value and encouraged his teams to listen before they spoke. Psychological safety became more than a theory – it became a daily practice. Microsoft's leadership did not just speak about inclusion, they modelled it.

One of the most powerful outcomes of this cultural shift was the creation of the Inclusive Design Toolkit a practical innovation designed to better serve people with disabilities. From that mindset came the Xbox Adaptive Controller, which allowed gamers with limited mobility to play with ease. But this innovation did not come from trying to "be diverse." It came from designing with belonging in mind.

The transformation was not top-down. Employees across departments were empowered to lead change from within. Employee Resource Groups became more than support spaces – they helped influence company policy, improve representation, and embed inclusion into the day-to-day.

The results spoke for themselves. Retention improved, innovation accelerated, and employees across Microsoft reported feeling more valued, more seen, and more heard.

This was not just a culture shift. It was a competitive advantage. A living example of what's possible when belonging becomes a company's foundation, not an afterthought.

Why belonging drives performance and innovation

Belonging is not just a moral imperative; it is a strategic one. When people feel they belong, they perform better, stay longer, and contribute more fully. Studies show that a strong sense of belonging can increase individual performance by over 50 percent. Inclusive teams are more innovative, more engaged, and more resilient. This is not theory, it is proven: organisations that prioritise belonging consistently outperform those that don't. When people feel seen, valued, and safe to be themselves, they do not just do their jobs, they do their best work.

Breaking the cycle of exclusion

Still, despite progress, everyday bias continues to erode belonging.

I have already mentioned how I have been mistaken for an assistant when I was the keynote speaker. At a corporate event, I was handed someone's coat, while everyone else was handed a champagne glass.

These moments may seem small, but they carry weight. They quietly tell you: *"You're not what we expected – and maybe, you do not belong here."*

Belonging is shaped in the smallest moments: who's acknowledged, who's interrupted, who's encouraged to speak. Culture is not what we declare. It is what we demonstrate daily. When people feel seen and safe in those moments, that is when they truly thrive.

Reflection Prompt

Where in your own life have you mistaken fitting in for belonging?

Have there been moments where you stayed silent, adapted, or held back to be accepted?

What would it look like to return to those spaces as your full self?

Call to Action

Embracing your own sense of belonging

Ask yourself honestly: Where do I feel most at home? Not just in a physical sense, but where do I feel safe, valued, and able to show up as my full self?

Then ask: How can I create more of those spaces, not just for me, but for others too?

Challenge the idea that you need to change in order to belong. Have you ever felt the pressure to fit in, to tone yourself down, or to hide part of who you are?

What would it mean to accept yourself completely, even the parts you were once told to minimise?

Reflect on your own journey. What pieces of yourself have you tucked away to make others comfortable? What would it look like to reclaim them?

Be the person who creates belonging for others.

Sometimes, all it takes is a kind word, an open invitation, or the courage to really see someone.

Ask yourself, "Who around me might be silently wondering if they belong? And what small action can I take today to help them feel included?"

Final Thought

Throughout my life, I searched for belonging as if it were something waiting for me out there in a place, a role, or someone else's approval. But the Arctic, my journey back to India, and every step since have taught me a deeper truth.

Belonging is not something we earn. It is something we remember. It is the quiet knowing that we are already enough.

You do not have to shrink yourself, bend your truth, or perform to deserve your place in the world. You belong simply because you are here.

And when you stand in that truth, you do not just find belonging for yourself, you create it for others too.

BEYOND THE ICE

Notes

CHAPTER 11

Legacy - Creating impact beyond ourselves

"I've learned that people will forget what you said, people will forget what you did, but people will never forget how you made them feel."
Maya Angelou

In a world that often celebrates speed, titles, and instant wins, legacy invites us to pause. To ask deeper questions. What will be your impact?

We often think of legacy as something that happens when we're gone, our name etched on a plaque, a title in a history book, or a list of achievements left behind.

But legacy is not about the end of the journey.

It is about the ripples we create every single day.

It is in the way we show up for others, the courage we inspire in them, and the impact we create, sometimes without even realising it.

What if your legacy is not something that happens later? What if it is happening right now?

BEYOND THE ICE

This chapter is not about how to be remembered. It is about making a difference now.

1. The Arctic - Carrying more than just our sleds

I went to the Arctic expecting a challenge: physically, mentally, and emotionally. I knew I would have to push myself, battle exhaustion, and navigate the unknown. What I did not expect was how much we would carry for each other.

At first, it seemed like we were each carrying only our own weight, our sleds filled with gear, food, and survival essentials. But as the days unfolded, it became clear we were carrying far more; one another's pain, vulnerability, and strength.

One evening, just as we had finished dinner, Belinda came running back into camp, tears streaming down her face. She had been gone for a while, and none of us had realised just how much she had been struggling. She was in pain, constipated, and suffering from cold-induced skin damage that made every movement unbearable.

It was a stark reminder of just how relentless the Arctic could be. Even basic human needs – finding food, getting rest, or relieving ourselves – became challenges that demanded courage and care.

But there was no hesitation. No embarrassment. No judgement. Just action.

We gathered around her, ensuring she was warm, reassuring her, and figuring out how to assist. Some of us distracted her with jokes to lighten the moment, while others quickly went into problem-solving mode, getting her into dry layers, making sure she was hydrated, and checking for any sign of frostnip damage.

She was not alone.

We weren't going to let her be.

Because legacy is not always about monumental acts or life-changing decisions.

Sometimes, it is about the people who see you in your most vulnerable state and do not turn away.

It is about creating an environment where no one feels ashamed to ask for help.

In leadership, in friendship, in life; our legacy is built in the moments where we show up for each other, without question.

2. The legacy of leadership - What they'll remember when you're gone.

I once worked with a senior leader who understood that authentic leadership is not about personal achievements; it is about who you lift along the way.

During a major organisational shift, she faced difficult decisions. Layoffs were inevitable, uncertainty was high, and morale was low. But instead of focusing only on keeping operations running smoothly, she prioritised supporting people through the transition.

She didn't just let go of employees. She mentored them, connected them with new opportunities, and helped them recognise their own strengths. She focused on building future leaders and left behind a culture equipped to thrive well after she had gone.

Years later, people still talk about her, not because of the position she held, but because of the way she led.

Some of her mentees went on to become leaders themselves, paying forward the lessons they had learned from her.

That is the kind of corporate legacy we should all strive for. It is not about how high we climb; it is about how many people we lift along the way.

Leadership that leaves a lasting mark

Authentic leadership is not about positions or control. It is about creating an environment where others can thrive, even in our absence.

3. Personal Legacy - Love, lessons, and quiet leadership

One of the most impactful leaders I ever worked with was not the loudest, the most senior, or the most decorated. He was the one who truly saw people.

One day, he asked me: "What do you want to create?"

He didn't tell me what success should look like for me. He did not push his version of achievement onto me. He simply created space for me to shape my own path.

For me, mutual trust and respect, integrity and authenticity have been at the heart of everything I have been fortunate enough to be able to influence. These values shaped how I showed up, how I led, and how I continue to support others to lead with intention.

That moment changed me.

If you are a leader, are you encouraging, enabling, and empowering those around you who may feel different, to capitalise on those differences and prevent them from holding themselves back?

And that is the essence of a great leader:

They leave people better than they found them. They create a culture where people feel empowered, seen, and valued. They do not just lead for today - they build a legacy that outlasts them.

Ask yourself:

What will my leadership leave behind? Am I creating space for others to grow, or am I solely focused on my own success?

Just as personal legacy lives in quiet moments of care, organisational legacy is shaped by the environments we create and the behaviours we model every day.

4. Above & Beyond Resilience - A case study in inclusive legacy

How inclusive leadership creates high-performing teams

A global client once approached me with a growing concern - their teams were diverse, but not inclusive. Employees from different backgrounds were part of the organisation, but they weren't contributing equally. The same voices dominated meetings, a select few were making key decisions, and some employees **felt invisible in the workplace.**

The leadership team was aware of the problem but did not know how to fix it. They had policies in place, they had attended unconscious bias training, but something was still missing - an active culture of inclusion at the leadership level.

Where my work made the difference

Instead of launching another generic diversity programme, I designed a targeted leadership intervention built around three core focus areas.

The first centred on **inclusive decision-making**. Leaders were supported to actively seek out diverse perspectives, ensuring that all voices were heard and considered before key decisions were made. This was not about token listening, it was about embedding different viewpoints into the very fabric of decision-making.

The second focus was on **team psychological safety**. Employees needed to feel safe enough to speak up, challenge ideas, and contribute fully. We worked together to design meeting structures that encouraged participation, particularly from quieter team members or those who had previously felt on the margins.

The final area was **inclusive leadership in action**. Through real-time coaching and feedback, leaders began shifting their behaviours, not through performance, but through presence. They started to show, not just say, that everyone mattered.

The results spoke for themselves. Within six months, team collaboration scores increased by 37 percent, with employees reporting that meetings felt more balanced, inclusive, and energised. Cross-functional innovation rose by 40 percent, as ideas that had once gone unheard were finally being acted upon. Even decision-making became faster, improving by 22 percent as teams drew on a wider pool of insight and expertise.

This case study reminds us that inclusion is not about optics or policies. It is about creating environments where everyone feels empowered to contribute. When leaders commit to that work not once, but consistently, the organisation doesn't just grow. It thrives.

Diversity & inclusion - A legacy beyond ourselves

For years, I struggled to find my place. I thought that if I could just work harder, prove myself more, I would earn my place.

But belonging is not something we should have to fight for. It is something we should build for others.

Diversity, inclusion, and representation are not about ticking boxes. They're about the legacy we leave for the next generation.

Who will see themselves in leadership because of you?

Who will feel included because you made space for them?

That is legacy.

Creating an Inclusive Legacy

Legacy lives in the way we advocate for others when they're not in the room. In the moments when we challenge assumptions and ask, *"Who is not being heard?"* Legacy grows every time we choose to mentor someone and help them believe in their own power.

BEYOND THE ICE

Everyday Legacy - The unseen ripple effect

Legacy is not only shaped in the extremes of the Arctic or the boardroom. It is built in the ordinary moments: the things we say, the way we listen, the choices we make when no one's watching.

It is the teacher who tells a child they believe in them. The colleague who notices when someone is quiet and checks in. The manager who gives someone their first real opportunity to shine.

We may never know the full impact of our actions, but that doesn't make them any less meaningful. Often, the legacy we leave is hidden in the stories others will one day tell:

"He made me feel like I mattered." "She helped me believe in myself." "They gave me a chance."

Your legacy might not be in headlines or history books. But it will live on in the confidence you helped someone find, the kindness you showed when it was needed most, and the door you held open for someone else to walk through.

That is how lasting change begins. One unseen ripple at a time.

Lessons to carry forward

I hope my family sees in me the power of courage, that taking risks, embracing the unknown, and standing up for what's right is always worth it, even when it is hard.

Whether it was crossing the Arctic in subzero temperatures, trekking Everest at high altitude, or pursuing challenges that seemed impossible, I hope they see that the greatest limits in life are often the ones we place on ourselves.

I hope they remember not just that we laughed, but that we laughed until our stomachs ached, until tears of joy ran down our faces.

That the warmth we shared was not just around the fireplace, eating our 'snicks snacks', but in the quiet, unspoken moments of trust, where they knew, they could come to me with anything.

That our conversations are a place where they can confide, seek advice, and feel safe in their most vulnerable moments, knowing that even if I do not always have all the answers, I am always willing to learn alongside them.

I hope they hold onto their values and ethics, even when the world around them doesn't.

That they understand success without effort may come easily to others, but actual achievement lies in knowing the work they put in themselves.

BEYOND THE ICE

Integrity is a quiet strength, and doing the right thing, especially when others don't, is its own greatest reward.

I hope they trust in their own abilities, that their self-worth is not dependent on the approval of others. Because true confidence doesn't come from external validation; it comes from within.

I hope they cherish the memories of our travels, the places we explored, and the adventures we embraced together. But more than that, I hope they cherish the love that is constant, the unfailing support that lets them grow, and the knowledge that no matter where life takes them, they will always have a home in my heart.

Because when we are together, the puzzle is complete.

Ultimately, my greatest legacy is not in my work, my words, or achievements. It is in the love I leave behind.

Your legacy starts now.

Your legacy is not something that begins one day in the distant future.

It starts in the choices you make today, in the way you show up for others, and in the impact you create, often without realising it.

When you help someone find their voice, you create a ripple effect that extends far beyond what you will ever see.
When you lift someone up in a moment of doubt, they carry that strength forward into their own journey.

When you challenge the status quo and advocate for change, you make it easier for others to step into their power.

We do not always see the mark we leave behind, but that doesn't mean it is not there.

Final Thought: The legacy you choose to build

What kind of legacy will you choose to create? What ripple effect will your actions set in motion? How will you use your voice, influence, and story to make a lasting impact?

Because legacy is not just about what we leave behind.

It is about how we shape the world today.

It is about the choices we make, the lives we touch, and the change we ignite.

And that starts now.

I hope my legacy is the same. That I too, can make people feel seen, valued, and loved, without conditions. Thank you, from the deepest part of my heart, to everyone who helped make this book and this journey possible. You are part of the legacy I carry forward.

Acknowledgements

No book is written alone, and this one would not exist without the support, love, encouragement, and wisdom of so many people along the way.

To my collaborators and clients who trusted me with their time and stories, thank you. Your insight, your questions, and your belief in this work pushed me to go further and dig deeper than I ever imagined.

To those who shared space with me in workshops, keynotes, and conversations, your openness gave these pages their meaning.

To those who took the time to read the early draft of this book, thank you for your insight, encouragement, and thoughtful reflections.

Sue, your feedback came back within days and helped shape the foundation of this work. Your observations challenged me to broaden my lens and consider experiences beyond my own. You reminded me that some stories speak for themselves and do not always need to be explained. Your reflections brought clarity and depth in ways I hadn't anticipated.

Gina, your voice notes or written comments after each chapter offered a consistent rhythm of encouragement and perspective. You asked thoughtful questions, highlighted areas that could be strengthened, and shared honest reactions that helped refine both the storytelling and the structure. Your presence was felt on every page.

Clinton, thank you for your attention to detail, reviewing the manuscript thoroughly, and helping ensure it was clean, original, and professionally presented. Your care and commitment added another layer of confidence to the final product.

Louis, thank you for your encouragement and belief in the message of this book. Sometimes, connection is the greatest form of feedback.

Hayley, thank you for your extraordinary foreword and the generous spirit behind it. Your words brought depth, clarity, and resonance to the heart of this book.

Thank you for walking beside me in the Arctic and beyond, and for showing up with such wisdom, integrity, and care. Your support, then and now, is part of the legacy I carry forward with gratitude.

And to **Karen**, my coach and grounding presence, thank you for holding space without pressure. You supported me with care, gave me the freedom to reflect at my own pace, and helped me find my voice again when I doubted it. Your wisdom and constant support have made all the difference.

My Greatest Legacy

Throughout this book, I have shared stories of leadership, belonging, and resilience. But if I could choose only one legacy to leave behind, it wouldn't be in my achievements. It would be in the love, strength, and wisdom I pass on to those around me.

I am who I am because of the people who have shaped me those who stood beside me, lifted me up, and believed in me even when I doubted myself.

I hope my family always knows that they are enough just as they are.

That they never feel the need to shrink themselves to fit into spaces that do not embrace them fully. That their voice, their dreams, and their kindness are their greatest strengths.

A love that grounds me

My husband has been my anchor, the steady presence through every triumph and every challenge. He has walked beside me in moments of uncertainty, never faltering in his belief in me. His love has been a constant reminder that true strength comes not from standing alone but from having someone who sees you thoroughly and completely and still chooses to stand by your side.

And then, there's Sabine

My best friend, my confidante, my soul sister. She has been a force of encouragement, pushing me to see my own worth when I couldn't, reminding me that I was capable of more. Through laughter, tears, and the countless moments that comprise a friendship, she has taught me that the right people in your life do not just support you, they challenge you to grow.

A family that chose me

When I married Matteo, I didn't just gain a partner, I gained a second family. My in-laws embraced me with love that knew no bounds, showing me what true parenting looks like. They never needed words to prove their care; they showed it through actions, kindness, and a depth of love that never diminished.

Through them, I learned that family is not defined by biology; it is defined by love, by the people who choose to stand by you, and by the bonds that grow stronger with time.

Epilogue

The journey that never really stopped

It is 2025. Ten years since I set off on a life-changing expedition to the Arctic.

Ten years since I pulled a 50kg sled across frozen terrain in -40°C temperatures, alongside twelve women I barely knew.

We trained for months, dragging tyres through muddy parks in all weather. We prepared not just our bodies, but our mindset. We were committed to something we believed in; challenging the status quo.

We spent so much time away from our families and friends to get fit and strong; not just individually, but as a group. Because in an environment like the Arctic, physical strength is only part of the story. Mental resilience, self-awareness, and trust in one another were equally essential. And yet, even with all that training, nothing could truly prepare us for the moment we stepped onto the ice.

The Arctic stripped away the noise and left only the truth of who we were, and who we were becoming.

What it gave me can't be measured in distance or degrees. It gave me clarity, courage, and a new definition of what's possible.

Earlier this year, several of us reunited. We decided to climb Pen y Fan. Although it is not as high as

Gunnbjørn Fjeld and the wind was only half as fierce as in the Arctic, it still challenged us more than expected. It was harder than expected, but just like on the ice, we made it together. Step by step.

We've all changed in the decade since that expedition. Some have launched businesses, changed careers, become mothers, relocated miles away... and one of us even wrote a book (Yes, that is me!).

But one thing is true for all of us - we've continued to grow. Facing the Arctic changed how I move through life. It taught me that growth comes not from ease, but from the courage to keep going.

The Arctic also revealed a side of me I hadn't known before - a taste for adventure, the courage to do hard and even wild things, like trekking to Everest Base Camp later this year, planning to climb Mount Kilimanjaro next, and walking sections of the Camino. Once you know you can survive the ice, you start to believe you can do anything.

If this book made you pause, reflect, or feel a little more seen, I'd love to hear from you. Do not hesitate to reach out and say hello!

And if you're looking for a keynote speaker, a facilitator, or a 1-to-1 coach to support your personal growth or a consultant to help your organisation build stronger leadership, inclusive cultures, or meaningful change, let's talk...

If you're ready to take your own reflections further, *"The Beyond the ice Journal: Reset, Rise and Repeat"* is also available to purchase. It is a space to pause, reconnect with yourself, and take purposeful steps forward.

Because the journey is not over.

It is only just beginning.

> *"You do not need to reach the summit to know you have grown. Often, it is in the climb itself, in the quiet courage to keep going, that we discover who we are becoming."*

BEYOND THE ICE

Connect with Leela

Email: leela.bassi@aboveandbeyond.ltd
LinkedIn: linkedin.com/in/leelabassi
Website: www.leelabassi.com
(use the QR code to visit the website)

To explore the companion...

Beyond the Ice Journal:

Reset, Rise and Repeat

...visit the website for more information and purchase options.

Printed in Dunstable, United Kingdom